About the Author

Guy Newmountain, aptly described by a former college tutor as a 'funnology', is a man who steadfastly resists categorisation. Artist, illustrator, animator and occasional DJ, he is, most notably, a teacher who has worked in over 100 different schools across the entire age range; with a breadth of experience rare in the profession. A guilty cola drinker with a fascination for contemporary fonts, TV title sequences, pioneering music videos and retro sci-fi, he swims a mile each weekday, grapples with a life-size Dalek and Wurlitzer jukebox and is rarely seen far from a black Labrador Retriever.

GUY NEWMOUNTAIN

Please I Can to the Toilet Go?

(The Memoirs of a Supply Teacher)

AUSTIN MACAULEY PUBLISHERS™

LONDON • CAMBRIDGE • NEW YORK • SHARJAH

A CIP catalogue record for this title is available from the British Library.

ISBN 9781035807987 (Paperback)
ISBN 9781035807994 (Hardback)
ISBN 9781035808014 (ePub e-book)
ISBN 9781035808007 (Audiobook)

www.austinmacauley.com

First Published 2023
Austin Macauley Publishers Ltd
1 Canada Square
Canary Wharf
London E14 5AA

Dedicated to those inspiring educators of my Primary, Middle and Secondary schooldays: Ujagar Singh Ahluwalia, Mike Gibby and Peter Twombley; my own family for their continued support whatever my endeavours, the countless, wonderful pupils I have had the honour of working with; and all those intrepid souls venturing boldly (or less so) into the supply teaching domain: do take my testimony with a hefty pinch of salt, for each of you I am sure will go on to forge your own successful, rewarding paths.

Acknowledgements

I would like to express my gratitude to Austin Macauley Publishers for indulging my idiosyncrasies as a first-time author and, most significantly, for granting me the freedom to use my own artwork throughout.

Contents

INTRODUCTION

To begin with – an admission. The sub-heading of this book is *partially* misleading. For the first eight years of my career, I wasn't yet a supply teacher: I did work in either permanent or long-term temporary posts; however, only until, having seen colleagues of mine weeping under the onslaught of paperwork, appraisals, observations, megalomaniac autocratic heads and OFSTED inspections, I became convinced that to continue would risk following suit, and perhaps even a breakdown. There's no way I would have reached

25 years in Education had I kept going. Rather than give up Teaching altogether, I moved sideways into supply; which did make up the vast majority (17 full years) of my service. Some of the anecdotes in this collection do, I confess, stem from the full-time days; but the lion's share honestly originated 100% in the supply domain!

Day-to-day supply, as any who have done it for even the briefest period will know, is a very strange, twilight life... You have to wake around 6-6.30 a.m., eat, wash and be dressed – ready to go out of the door by 7; any time after which, agencies or schools may begin calling. Part of you desperately wants the telephone to ring so that you can earn some much needed cash; the other part dreads it doing so, as you would just love to spend the day at home relaxing, catching up on tasks undone and enabling your voice to recover – meaning you almost jump out of your very skin when it does suddenly ring. Invariably, it's hit rush-hour, the roads are gridlocked with the school-run and they want you there 20 minutes ago! Even with children already through the school door, those calls can still happen: a teacher came into work but has suddenly come over funny and can't complete the day, etc. So you do tend to run much of the time on adrenalin...

Sat Nav, or the iPhone's Maps app *revolutionised* getting to work in the morning; prior to that, navigation was simply you and a battered A-Z, meaning frequent perilous stops in lay-bys to figure out where on earth you were. On the darkest winter mornings it used to be a case of resorting to reading the numbers glowing white on wheelie-bins! But of course, the Satnavs are not infallible, I was once told "You have reached your destination," having been sent up a muddy dirt track to a gated field, "The Smithy"... Another time I ended up in a cul-de-sac of residential houses, no school in sight. Often the BBC English automated voice in your earpiece will tell you: "In a quarter of a mile, the destination is on your right" – when in fact it is on your left, and vice-versa – an imperfect science at best.

I don't know anyone who has done supply anywhere near as long as I did. I worked in a total of 130 Leicester schools, with every age from Foundation 1 to A2. I suppose I must have seemed a bit of a cartoon character: I had a belt with my first name on the brass buckle, a succession of metallic silk shirts every colour of the rainbow; and, as my surname was rather a mouthful, the children just called me "Mr Guy" – it's short and quick; and many would nostalgically continue to use it even when they re-encountered me in Secondary school.

99% of my work was in Primary; Secondary's great if you have a specialism; but behaviour-wise, when things kick off at that level, they are much trickier to defuse! Via General Cover, I taught almost every subject. I was quite a difficult ol' codger by the end, with much I wouldn't do, only because tough experience taught me I had to be consistent or agencies would take liberties. (They still rule the roost in supply, have done for over 20 years now and desperately need regulating; Council-run supply pools are, by and large, a thing of the past). The agencies all knew 9.15 a.m. was my absolute cut-off; you have to put your foot down or you'll be amazed how late you can sometimes be called; which means you cannot plan your day...) I would only work Full Days, never Half, because by the time they've taxed you it's barely worth it; plus, once it's known you will do half-days, that's likely to be all you'll get offered. Same as qualified teachers agreeing in desperation to go in as a T.A (Teaching Assistant) for half the pay – once the agencies know you can be persuaded to do that, you'll be lucky to get Teaching assignments ever again. Other staff may thrive on "challenging" environments; I personally wouldn't get out of bed for any "war-zone." And I would only travel within a 10 mile radius of my postcode, otherwise you can spend a sizeable chunk of your earnings on petrol – very, very seldom do they give you a fuel allowance.

If you are willing to relax some of these criteria you will get offered infinitely more work; bear in mind though that much of it will be further out than you would like and in the tougher schools. Day-to-day supply's not for everyone, you have to be highly tolerant of uncertainty, both in your working day and income-wise. There can be long spells without work. Insist at the time of registration on being paid P.A.Y.E (it is *always* possible), and avoid "umbrella" payroll schemes like the plague: if the agency's name is not on your payslip, but another company's, that means payroll has been outsourced to a third party; the agency doing that will give you all the assurances under the sun that you will be 'X' pounds a year better off if you go down this route, but it can cause trouble with HMRC. Expect to be paid way below your rightful place on the Teacher's Pay Spine... and if you are sole earner, with a family to support, the regularity of work is just too unreliable. You do have to consider your financial future seriously.

Due to the agencies not being set up to contribute to the Teacher's Pension Scheme (TPS), for a 25-year career in Teaching, I have just 8 years of pension contributions. That's including a transfer-*in* of a private pension plan (*very* reluctantly granted as a one-off.) Although nowadays, agencies are obliged to offer the Workplace Pension, you will almost certainly end up with tiny pockets of badly underperforming pension schemes all over the place that you'll have to keep note of; and eventually combine. I worked for 14 agencies and joined many, many more who never got me a single day's work: bags of hot air run by 20-something college graduates! They fold, move cities or the two of you part ways all the time...

But income aside, the plus points of supply *far* outweigh the bad. You get a fabulous breadth of experience, right across the age range if you choose. I know staff who have never stepped out of one school their entire career – they train there, get taken on and never leave. I even overheard one such person say, *"What Mr Guy does is my idea of Hell..."* I would argue that it wasn't until I stepped *out* of a familiar, safe situation that I gained a valuable sense of perspective and realised how much extra I'd been expected to take on; and actually, how exploited my goodwill had been!

I do hope that you enjoy the stories within: they span my entire career. In one or two I've truly bared my soul; put my hands up to painful mistakes I made that others should learn from. Some moments were happy, others sad; some were deadly serious, others absolute *howlers*. The cover title itself was inspired by one such event. In one of my earliest Reception classes, we used a structurally sound, but now somewhat dated reading scheme called *1,2,3 and Away.* The 4+ children were first introduced to the book characters by way of a box of finger-puppets and large A3 laminated posters of each person; one of whom, Mrs Blue-hat, stood out from the rest and particularly seized the classes' imagination. In all the other posters, the characters had cartoon smiles; but Mrs Blue-hat, under her Quality Street-style parasol, was notoriously strict and bad-tempered, with a frown and downturned mouth. I used to save that card until the very last, putting it at the very back of the pile, because I knew how eager all the children were, waiting to see it.

There was an incredibly earnest Foundation 2 child who would plunge his hand as high as he could into the air, gasping and spluttering in his urgency to give the answer: "Miss-Miss-Mrs BLUE-HAT!" Many of these tiny children had English as a second language:

you laughed with them, but never *at* them – however one day, shortly after we had been reinforcing toilet etiquette, this same boy accosted me suddenly:

"Mr Guy, I wanto sh*t!"

"No – you don't use that word in school... now come on – ask properly."

To which he responded, with the most urgent, lip-trembling, eager-to-please expression:

"Please-I-can-to-the-toilet-go?"

I was literally doubled-up in laughter, he had tried so very hard – it was all I could do to gesture with my hand and wave him consent!

For any readers considering a career in Education, *all* teachers experience precious, unique, unpredictable and *priceless* moments like this. *Write them down* – they will brighten even your darkest hour; as will keeping a large envelope of "Thank you" cards, letters and even grateful post-its to look back on during less positive days, when you might be questioning the impact of the contribution you make. There is no feeling better than those rare occasions when you catch a fleeting glimpse of yourself operating really well as a teacher; secure in your knowledge, well-prepared and a class in the palm of your hand, responding to you positively and hanging on your every word. On the other hand, it's not a career for the faint-hearted: when you *do* have a bad day, there is virtually nothing as bad as a bad day in Teaching – any humiliation involved can be very public indeed... But trust me, those days are mercifully few and far between!

To preserve the anonymity of all pupils and staff featured, I have purposely kept most individual names and locations out of this book. You might by chance pick up the odd tip here or there, but please don't expect to find schemes of work galore or a goldmine of behaviour management strategies – I was never that good in either of those spheres! – besides, there are plenty of other sources of such information. What *is* my aim is simply to share with you a highly varied collection of real-life anecdotes – all *absolutely* true – which might give you some indication of what it's like to be the other side of that desk: the craziest ups and downs, the best times and the worst, in a career like no other – the working life of a supply teacher.

BOOM! SHAKE THE LESSON-PLAN

My first ever teaching job after qualifying in 1993 wasn't actually in my home town, but way down south in a secondary school in Aylesbury, Buckinghamshire. It was just a half-term stint to cover an Art teacher's maternity leave, but it gave me a taster of what real Teaching would be like; and I had a lively tutor-group of shrieking, hormonal Year 10's, all of whom I bought huge doughnuts when I left. The school had caught fire a few years before; and this giant of a Headteacher had gone back into the building in search of any pupils; he had third degree burns all down one side of his body; and, in his office, a huge tapestry of The Sealed Knot – an association dedicated to costumed re-enactments of the English Civil War.

He was very much "old-school" in his thinking and often found himself on the wrong side of the female staff; having particularly offended one woman teacher who had come into school wearing trousers rather than a skirt. Looking her up and down, his verdict was, "No wonder your husband divorced you." You'd get done for that now... He made it clear to me on my first visit that staff were expected to dress to a high standard; I think it was the only time in my life that I regularly visited a dry-cleaner. The Head was pleased; telling me I was "a credit to the school."

My lodgings down there were really not great: I lived in a tiny box room with a single bed, under the sloping rafters of a small detached house owned by a young African-Caribbean man, who was letting it to pay the mortgage. Apart from me, the only other long-term, regular occupants of the house were a 17-year-old couple who had run away from their parents to consummate their teenage love. It's no exaggeration to say they were at it like *rabbits*.

I happened to get a half-day once; and came home at lunchtime to find the walls shaking, the sound of them screaming out in passion and the squeaking springs of their bed clearly audible through the wafer-thin wall, as they played their favourite track on a loop: the current Number One by D.J. Jazzy Jeff and Fresh Prince, *Boom! Shake the Room!* They were certainly giving it their best shot. Periodically the cassette single would run out and all canoodling would cease temporarily as one of them scuffled out of bed to switch it over; no sooner would the music resume, than the screams and grunts of ecstasy would also. Well within earshot in my squalid, adjacent digs, it made it very hard indeed for me to focus on my lesson plans.

A REAL-LIFE CINDERELLA STORY

One afternoon, I was teaching a group of Foundation 2 pupils at "carpet-time" at the end of the day; and telling the Slovakian story of Budulinek, an all-time class favourite after which I later named a new black Labrador puppy. Midway through the fairy-tale, out of the corner of my eye, I vaguely registered a little girl a couple of rows back, fiddling with something in her hand which she had brought to the carpet. Although not a thing she should have been doing, it was hardly exactly naughty: many small children (and I was one of them) find some small piece of classroom equipment fascinating, or keep a comfort item with them for security. But it was distracting others nearby – and me – from the story. Well, so used to similar occurrences was I that I did not even look her way (*that* would teach me)... Continuing to tell the tale, I just automatically reached out to the girl, firmly clicked my fingers, opened my hand, she put whatever the item was in my palm, I closed it and went on reading.

You must please believe me when say I truly intended to give this unknown object back to the child concerned at Home Time – but so many other things were happening. It's a fairly fraught period on most days: letters and paintings to give out, shoelaces to tie, coats to zip up, doors to open, etc. that it completely slipped my mind. At some random point, while focused on other tasks, I must have sensed clutter in my hand, it found its way into my pocket and I deposited the artefact there... It wasn't until I got home, and felt something unexpected among the coins, whistle, and keys, that I pulled out the object to investigate – only to discover the most beautifully-sequined, miniature pink felt bag – with *something* inside... Curiously, I reached down into its depths and my fingers met something smooth, shiny and cool... a tiny, golden horseshoe; plastic for sure, but without doubt, that little child's personal treasure!

I felt awful then. In my conscience, that small girl was lying awake at night, crying for her lost charm. Perhaps the bag had even been made for her by her Grandma. The guilt ate away at me. There and then, I made a firm commitment in my mind to return the magic horseshoe to its expectant owner the very next time I visited that school. Which was bound to be the next day – wasn't it?

By way of an explanation for the delay which followed, these were the halcyon days of supply teaching. There was no shortage of work and I could quite easily visit five different schools in the same week. I thought I must soon get an assignment back at that particular one – but the days went by, then the weeks; and the months. Always, I kept the little bag at the bottom of my 'To Do' chest, fully meaning to do the right thing. Periodically, whenever I cleared out unwanted paperwork, I came across it. I knew I should take the time to call in at the school, just to return the little horseshoe. But my life was busy; and I kept forgetting. And the *years* passed...

Then – finally – after three or four had gone by, I got the call to go back to that very same Primary school... No way was I going to squander the opportunity! Arriving at the staffroom, I approached the Headteacher, told her the tale and asked if, with her permission, I might please have just a couple of minutes in front of the whole school at the end of Assembly. She loved the account and was more than happy to comply.

"This is a *real-life* Cinderella story..." I began, ending the description of what had happened with the words, "I am going to leave this bag with your Headteacher. Whoever it is that can knock on her door and tell her correctly what the secret object is inside, it will be returned to you..."

Within an hour, the Head entered my classroom, delighted to inform me that the identity of the little girl to whom the horseshoe belonged had been confirmed. It turned out that her family had in fact moved house and she had left the school a couple of years earlier! But her closest friend, who had sat next to her on the carpet back then, had remembered the incident clearly, a formative memory indeed; and the school had all the necessary contact details. I genuinely felt a weight had been lifted: *Laura* – from the bottom of my heart, I am sorry! A teacher's wrong, eventually righted – owner and treasure reunited...

CHALLENGING BEHAVIOUR

Arriving early one day at one of the city's rougher community colleges, my early misgivings were borne out.

First instruction received: "Lock your car." An ominous portent of what was to come.

The place was like a prison: electronic locks halfway up corridors, even a barrier dividing one half of the *staffroom* from the other, requiring a swipe key to get through.

I had to supervise the wildest English lesson. I got the distinct impression I was just the latest in a whole succession of supply teachers covering this class. The video left for me, a dated black and white 1930's movie adaptation of *An Inspector Calls,* was insufficient to hold the group and within a couple of minutes, they began chucking pencil crayons... Before I knew it, the air was full of a hail of missiles being pelted back and forth, sharp points outwards.

Ducking the violently thrown objects, I raised my voice: "Right – pack it in!"

To no avail.

A mouthy African-Caribbean girl, clearly the ringleader, spotted the Loblan cowboy boots under my trousers and yelled:

"*DON'T* you tell us what to do! *LOOK* a' you – look a' you – in yo' *FOCKIN'* Long-Johns!"

Which brought the whole class down – they collapsed in laughter. Even though it was at my expense, and highly inappropriate for her to speak to any teacher that way, I had to suppress my own mouth twitching in amusement: you had to be in the situation – something about it was quite funny.

Fortunately, Senior Management arrived at that point and control was restored for the remainder of the lesson.

Later, between classes, I encountered that student again in the corridor. With a look of exultant triumph, she shouted, "You got *RIPPED*... You got ripped *GOOD!*"

I survived the full week's assignment there; but came out of it feeling as if I had been pulled through a hedge backwards; and although I vowed not to return, you can only say "no" to so many assignments before an agency get fed up with you. One day, some 10 years later, after work had been scarce for a while, I rashly felt obliged to go back to the same location. Despite a lavish new build, behaviour was unchanged. Worst of all, I was supposed to be doing General Cover when in fact the whole day, bar Period 4, was Drama. I was also the third different supply teacher the students had had in a row since their previous regular teacher gave up.

The workspaces were huge and very tricky to manage; one was separated from the corridor outside only by a black curtain, which passing students could rip open and drag along whilst yelling insults through to disrupt the lesson. As I was at one end of the space, they could rush the lights at the other; and repeatedly plunge the entire room into darkness. The stepped behaviour management strategy was woefully ineffective; finally a 7-foot bearded behemoth on the Behaviour Mentoring team responded to the din, burst in and bawled them (temporarily) into submission; though of course, in-so-doing he had fatally undermined any vestige of authority I may (to that point) have had left. The only light relief was a Year 11 PSHE lesson; in which most of the students were revising.

However, this was a college in which they were allowed their mobile phones out. Before long, I heard a loud, robotic computer-simulated phone's voice: "Guy...Guy..." I used "tactical ignoring." Getting no response from me, the perpetrators then turned the focus of their vitriol on each other, until the electronic voice was uttering, "I'm coming! I'm coming! Inside Connor!" – and that – trust me – was the easiest lesson of the day. Though I did earn every penny of my cut-rate pay, on the plus-side, I was out, free, into bright sunshine at 2.30 p.m. – and I *never* made the mistake of going there a third time!

SNAKES IN A CLASSROOM

Booked for a day in a large, busy comprehensive (long since demolished and rebuilt to wondrous standards), I found myself teaching
Humanities to Years 7, 8 and 9 in the most remote upstairs classroom
in the school... The memory is vivid for several reasons: the first

being that as I opened the desk drawer in search of a ream of lined paper, I found article after newspaper article about dangerous snakes. It was clear that the class teacher had something of an obsession about them. Then I spotted the large glass, bulb-lit cage at the back of the room, a two-storey den containing a coiled-up boa constrictor of some considerable girth. This was no wiry, slender little garter snake – the thing had major width and substance...but the glass barrier ensured we were safe – or so I thought...

The second notable memory about that day is that one period had the distinction of being the only cover lesson I *ever* refused, on principle, to teach. The pupils were studying World War 2 and in particular the rise of the Third Reich. The class teacher had, I am sure – at least I hope! (rather than think him a sympathiser) – the best of motives for the work he rather naively set: for the students to design a poster encouraging citizens to join the Nazi party... I just could not bring myself to deliver that lesson... Had even one student got the wrong idea and been left with the impression there was something positive about Adolf Hitler and his murderous mob, that would have been one too many; and I had no interest in potentially steering their minds in an extreme right-wing direction. So I just chose to muddle through and skip that task as best I could, setting them alternative work from the textbook.

Thirdly, from the moment one of the afternoon classes entered the room, there was friction between a number of the girls and an atmosphere you could cut with a knife. Before long, a shouting match blew up between several of them, one of whom burst into floods of tears and had to be taken outside the room to calm down. In between sobs, she explained that several of the girls, including her, had had a sleepover the previous weekend; and that apparently her pyjamas were not seen as up to the latest fashion and had been ridiculed by the others. The disagreement had spread to parental involvement level and now several of the parents had fallen out. The class was so high on the tension that the lesson was barely teachable – I had to send for an on-call member of staff, who did not arrive after the first message was sent. Another more reliable pupil had to be dispatched before anyone turned up to settle them – by which time most of the lesson was over!

As the class exited the room like a hurricane leaving a battered town, I moved from area to area collecting the various debris the students had left behind, both on and under the tables. My eyes happened to fall on the snake cage – only to see a two-and-a-half inch gap between the glass and the metal frame – it was open... It had not even been locked – or if it had, one of the students had got hold of the key from the desk drawer during all the distraction and slid the glass to one side... Fortunately, the occupant was still incarcerated, but it had uncoiled and its forked tongue was flicking visibly from side to side. To have been strangled by a ravenous boa constrictor would not have been an auspicious end to the day, and somewhat beyond the normal experience your average supply teacher might expect on a typical assignment. Never a dull moment...

THE QUEEN'S DRINK

When my little brother and I were tiny boys, we used to play a childish game of "drinking like the Queen drinks" – of course we had no idea how she really drank, but in our infant imaginations, instead of just raising the glass to her lips in a straightforward manner, she swung it from side to side in very grand, ever-narrowing spirals until the liquid within it reached the required destination...

After many years' teaching, my voice began to show the strain, and in fact reached a very serious point by my early 40's in which it felt – literally – as if I had a pigeon-ring around my throat – it was in constant tension, making the simplest act of swallowing difficult. I even had to go to a wonderful lady in Market Harborough, who inhabited an extraordinary room decorated like that of a wizard, for voice therapy. She made me lie on the floor and taught me some useful strategies to minimise voice strain. There were many options, from ensuring correct posture to tongue, jaw and voice "stretches" prior to teaching: "*Maaa, May, Me, My, More...*" – but the one which helped the most on a day-to-day basis was simply always to have a bottle of honey dissolved in hot water with me, from which, unapologetically, I would swig regularly.

Well, all the kids now have water bottles in the classroom, so why on earth should teachers have to wait for a coffee break to wet their whistles? It did begin as fresh lemon and honey, and the kids used to watch with fascination "ooyah!"-ing with delight as the pips I deliberately left in the bottle floated up and down inside the glaucous liquid like a diving bell; or hung mid-bottle like a spirit balance. I'm sure plenty of regular staff, resentful of my supply freedom, must have sneered at "Mr Guy and his little bottle of wee" behind my back; but the acid in the lemon began to strip the lining off my throat; and after abandoning its use (I hear ginger is very good), I found honey alone perfectly sufficient.

I happened to go to a school one day with the sweetest Year 1 autistic girl in the class. You would never have known there was anything unusual about her, except that if all the class were sitting on the floor in a circle at carpet time for a learning or listening activity, she would be sitting quietly facing the *wrong* way out of the circle... The class teacher had done a great job of making laminated photos of the little girl joining in each of her school subjects; and the relevant picture would be displayed in each lesson to encourage her participation. The girl seemed to take great interest in my bottle of drink. Suddenly, for no apparent reason, the childhood game came back to me. "Do you want to see how the Queen drinks?" I asked her, as the rest of the class watched.

She nodded eagerly. "Well first, this is how Mr Guy drinks," I said seriously, and took a small swig in an ordinary fashion, "but when the QUEEN drinks," I went on, "because she's the Queen, she drinks like this..." – I had that class spellbound as the bottle swung in spirals towards my mouth. "Do you want to see it again?" I asked.

"Yes!" they shouted, so I went through it all again in what was to become a familiar and much-loved ritual..."Okay, so this is how Mr Guy drinks" (note my referring to myself in the third person for extra dramatic emphasis), "...but when the Queen drinks, she drinks like this..." to lots of delighted laughter. Lord knows how many of them went home that night and told their parents that's how the Queen really drank!

Well, I forgot all about that episode until, around three years later, I was asked back and taught the little autistic girl's class again – and the first, the very first thing she said was, "Mr Guy, will you show us how the Queen drinks?"

So it stuck and was a very good ice-breaker, never ceasing to fascinate the children whenever I was introducing myself to a class of smaller ones. Although there *was* one class who became totally obsessed with it. Over a longer two-week assignment covering for a teacher who was off suffering with a chipped coccyx, I made the mistake of introducing, a few days in, how the *King* drinks. (With a deep "Aaaah" at the end and the spirals going the opposite way). At their insistence, we then had to invent how the *Prince* drinks (the bottle bouncing and him shouting "Prince-ky Korsakoff!" after the swig) and finally the *Princess*, whose bottle swoops down from above to a little "Ohhh!" afterwards). All of which took way too long to be educational and had to be knocked on the head.

Silly Mr Guy... But to this day, I still have children coming up to me begging, "Will you show us how the Queen drinks?"

DISRESPECT TO THE LAST PLANTAGENET

During an all-too-brief year working in the private sector, I was given the option to leave my vehicle in a tiny, exclusive private car park belonging to the senior school opposite. Bang in the centre of the city and off-limits to the general public, it was only accessible via the narrowest of one-way alleys – you could barely call it a street! Staff working in the Junior school where I was, several miles away, were still entitled to the same parking permissions and could use the miniature car park whenever they wanted.

I took advantage of the opportunity on several occasions when making carefree, last-minute shopping trips into town, just before the shops closed. Whenever I did, I always favoured a particular spot in that car park – little knowing that, *directly* under my own car wheels, buried for 530 years, (and only shock-revealed by archaeologists 10 years later in 2012), was the yet-to-be-discovered skeleton, complete with widely-documented scoliosis of the spine, of the last Plantagenet King of England, Richard III... No disrespect intended, Your Majesty.

BINKY-BOO

I would often find myself teaching mixed-year Primary classes; and in one such group was a small girl whose name was... well, let's just say it began with a letter 'B.' When I came to her name in the register, I read it out aloud just as I saw it – however I was imme-diately corrected by the class T.A. Apparently, said child's parents had come into the school to *insist* that all staff only address their daughter as "Binky-Boo." Talk about wrapping your child in cotton-wool! Now you might think this was one of those children who are much "younger," behaviour-wise than their peers; who needed more frequent reassurance; and that butter wouldn't melt in her mouth – but no: she was a right devious, defiant and challenging little tearaway, who clearly had one 'act' for school, another for home – and both parents wrapped around her little finger!

EMBARRASSING MOMENTS

Whilst teaching Graphics at a well-known high-achieving community college, I was often required to mentor PGCE students, giving them constructive written feedback on their performance after each observation had ended. One later turned out to be an art fraudster in a highly-publicised case; and was jailed for his forgeries before becoming a reformed character and turning his fortunes around. In their first sessions the PGCE students allocated to me would come into my own lessons purely to watch and pick up on as much classroom management as they could. During one such period, while I was giving the initial lesson introduction to the students, I caught sight of a pair of the visitors giggling uncontrollably at the back of the room. This I did my best to ignore for some time, until finally, with their laughter becoming contagious, I challenged them in sheer bewilderment: *"What?"*

Whereupon one of them kindly came over and whispered under her breath, "You're flying low."

Mortified, I manfully made light of the news; said, *"Now* I know what PGCE students are for!" corrected my zip and moved on fast. I can only imagine the mirth at my expense when they reported that anecdote back at teacher training college!

But worse was to come...

One fateful morning, I made the fashion error of dressing in a pair of trousers which must have shrunk in the wash... A bachelor, unversed in the skills of using the correct machine settings for different fabrics, I tend to bung everything in together; and so this is an occupational hazard which occurs with some regularity... Bending down during a free period to pick up a dropped project folder, I heard a loud "r-r-RIP!" sound. It was classic Laurel and Hardy – fumbling behind me with an awful sinking feeling, I was appalled to find the tightly stretched fabric had given out precisely in the crotch-seam region. With no jumper, jacket or cardigan to cover the fact, I could only hope that no-one would notice – but I was not aided by the fact that, underneath the black trousers, I had on a pair of neon green boxers – the contrast was unmissable. Within minutes my pretty, eagle-eyed Sicilian colleague slunk alongside me, whispering in her sly tones, "You do know you've split your trousers?"

"Errrrr yes – I'm aware of that fact," I replied stiffly, mustering as much dignity as I could in my profuse embarrassment.

There was no time to return home for a change of clothing – the bell had rung for Period 3: my merciless and untameable Year 11 Graphics group. There was nothing for it but to position myself on a stool before the class began and stay firmly seated the entire double lesson... But one sardonic student had beaten me to it, and before I could reach the security of the stool, I heard her shriek delightedly to her approaching friend, "EEER HHEEEER! Sir's split 'is trousers!"

I started laughing uncontrollably despite myself.

"Sir! Stand up sir, stand up!" she snickered as the rest of the class filtered in, but petrified of being made a laughing-stock and the subject of mocking gossip the entire school over, I refused to budge; and, only via a stern tone of voice hinting at unpleasant detention consequences, did I manage to subdue the girl from pursuing her juvenile intimidation.

It was unheard of and highly uncharacteristic for me to stay in one position for the entire duration of a double lesson: my teaching method was one of more-or-less constant movement around any group, to the point where one student had even remarked, "Sir, you remind us of a circling shark, the way you circle around us..." So the group was puzzled and suspicious, to say the least, by my sudden immobility.

After what seemed an eternity, the lunchtime bell finally went and I dismissed the class. I waited for every one of the mass of students to exit the open-plan classroom – and only when it seemed the coast was one hundred percent clear, did I furtively rise from the safety of the stool, heavy files in hand, to begin the perilous hundred-yard journey to the security of the Design staffroom.

But I had not walked even 10 metres when I heard a jubilant scream, "*EEER!* HEH HEH HEH!"

The same girl, along with her best friend, had seized the opportunity to hide behind a white display plinth in the neighbouring classroom: they had ringside seats for my humiliation, as, between spasms of laughter, I sidled like a crab from side to side, trying to conceal my green boxers from their merciless eyes... thank goodness it was before the era of camera phones – I would have been posted up on YouTube before the day was out!

THE EGG AND SPOON RACE

My first-ever 4+ Reception class in January 1994 was, by today's standards, a rarity. It wasn't by any means a small class, with around 27 Foundation 2 pupils; but nowadays, it's common to find well over 30 in a class. What *was* remarkable about it was the *complete* absence of any child with Special Needs – that is something virtually unheard of today, when there is always at least one, if not several such children in every class. Mine was a 100% Asian population in which English was very much a second language; so although gesture made up a large amount of our early communication, because of their high ability level, it was possible, whilst hearing them read one at a time, to bring all the children in the class up together on the *same* reading book, with none of them falling behind – a phenomenon I never experienced again for the rest of my teaching career.

The room itself was the only real disadvantage. Prior to Christmas, there had been trouble with a neighbour who lived across the road. He had been a long-running nuisance, in conflict with the school over this and that for some time. Although it couldn't be proven, he was strongly suspected to be responsible for an arson attempt on my classroom during the holidays: something alight had been pushed in from the outside; and while the fire didn't spread beyond that room, the walls were charred and blackened. They had been neatly repainted before the children ever set foot inside, but nonetheless, the smoke was fixed in the walls underneath the new paint; which meant by the end of every day, your throat felt as if it was on fire from inhalation!

That aside, it was a wonderful year. The boys in the class were vastly outnumbered by the girls: there were only seven of them, six of whom were fiercely competitive Alpha-male types: confident, pushy and physical; however one little boy was much smaller and more gentle. Over a period of time observing and monitoring him, it became clear that this child was hyper-focused: while he couldn't match the prowess of the other boys in physical tasks (in fact, he often fell short and was left behind, or got shoved out of the way); he more than surpassed them academically, with a serious manner and high intelligence making him stand out from the rest.

Towards the end of the Summer Term, Sports Day beckoned, with parents invited to come and watch. Each child had to be included in a race with children from other classes; and it was down to the teachers to assign them to the different activities. I had no concerns at all about the other six boys: all were either strong or fast runners and I had no doubt they would do well in their events; so I readily allocated races and relays for them. The smallest boy, however, I *was* worried about. He wasn't fast or particularly able physically, and the last thing I wanted was for him to be humiliated before his parents; to come last and be shown up in front of his peers. For all I knew, that could be the start of a lifelong sense of failure and low self-esteem. What could I do? But then again, there was that nagging reminder of a searing intellect, that intense focus and particular drive about him. If *only* that gift could be harnessed somehow, he had a good chance of smashing the competition... And then I realised exactly where he belonged: the perfect fusion between boy and category... The Egg and Spoon Race!

Well, the big day came and much to my delight, all the other six boys in my class won their races hands down. Only one left to go. As all the children lined up, spoons outstretched, there was that look on the boy's face, rigid with concentration. I could have been forgiven for imagining a bead of perspiration trickling from his brow as I watched, transfixed, as the whistle blew to signify the start.

While others in the race dropped their eggs, picked them up, replaced them in the spoons, then dropped them again, with impeccable balance and poise, not a wobble in sight, he was first across the finish line. I felt my chest swell up – I was so proud of the little fella I could have cried. That result meant more to me than any other win that afternoon. He hadn't done better than his own class peers, he'd just come equal. But what he hadn't done was fall behind them. And that is what it means as a teacher to really come to 'know' any child in your care: to identify their individual assets, then channel those strengths in the right directions to ensure you get the very best from them.

ASPERGER'S ANECDOTE

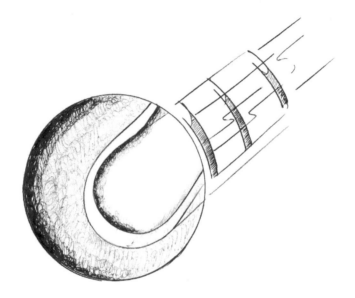

I once taught a Year 10 student whose reputation preceded him. Staff were tipped off in advance at a special S.E.N. meeting that, with a diagnosis of Asperger Syndrome, he may prove tricky to deal with. That turned out to be an understatement. The lad was actually quite low in self-esteem, and needed regular reassurance that he wasn't in trouble; but all that was eclipsed by his being decidedly menacing, at around 6 feet tall, with a sinister habit of staring directly at me with a frozen gaze. If ever I asked him what he was doing, the answer would invariably be, "Calling you a freak."

And if you asked him to do anything specific, you would often get the response, "How about *No*?"

He seemed to pop up everywhere: when I was in town shopping, even when I was walking my Labrador miles out in the country-side along the canal. He would spring out of nowhere, seize and hold to ransom my dog's tennis ball and yell out over a bridge, *"Newmountain!"*

The first six months or so were quite a trial until he got used to me; then he began showing more interest in actually getting a grade in my subject. His attendance was sporadic and he was never one to accomplish much in lesson time, so for a short period, I tutored him one-to-one after school; although to get his worksheets done, I more or less had to dictate to him each sentence he wrote. He gave up on the extra sessions after only two or three, then one day, he asked me in a confidential tone, "Realistically, sir, what grade do you think I could get in Graphics?"

I thought about it, and then decided it would be unfair to raise the lad's hopes falsely, only for them to be dashed at results time, so I answered, "Realistically? I think an 'E'."

I was expecting him to be disappointed and to respond resentfully, so was quite surprised by his response:

"Sir, do you know," he said, "If I get an 'E' for Graphics, I'll be coming to shake your hand."

And sure enough, on GCSE Results Day, he came across to me, beaming: "Sir, I got my 'E'!"

That student was a success story. To him, his 'E' grade meant as much as an 'A' would to most of his peers. He left, I think, to join a special hands-on vocational apprenticeship-type course up north. I genuinely wish him all the best.

INNOVATION

There was a bespectacled student in one of my Year 11 groups who was argumentative, noisy and did next to no work in my subject. However, he had a reputation throughout his Year-group for being blisteringly intelligent, so my lessons must have been at fault not to hold him! For his Graphics Major Project, he had chosen to make a Point-of-Sale display stand, to promote *what* exactly, I forget. It was a group I had inherited from a previous teacher when joining the college; and the sum total this student had produced, in months, was a rubber Marigold glove, crudely painted black and stuck on top of an upturned cardboard box.

I had just taken the Register, given a brief intro and released the class to work on their individual making tasks, when, seconds later, he yelled out, "Sir! Have you got any glue?"

With the benefit of hindsight, I should have decanted some for him, anticipating that students of that age are unpredictable in every respect; but there was a barrage of noise and activity in the room, I was in a lot of demand simultaneously and I just pointed him in the direction of a new, full container of Marvin Medium standing by the sink in the corner; before my attention was diverted by the needs of another student.

When I turned back in his direction, to my horror, he had poured the entire contents of that 5-litre PVA tub (which under ordinary circumstances should have lasted the best part of a *term)* over his glove and cardboard stand: to say the gloopy coating was an inch thick is no exaggeration. The resulting mess from the heavy rivulets overflowing onto both the desk and the floor must have been a joy for the cleaners to behold that night...

But the irony is, that several weeks later, when it was brought down from its drying refuge high up on top of a glass display case, the stand, I must confess, did look quite *cool*. The glue had dried to be entirely clear, giving the black glove preserved deep underneath a futuristic, science-fiction-like – even kinky appearance! Brilliance can take many forms, so perhaps the famous saying is correct:

"Innovation...takes the unreasonable mind."

THE DEATH THREAT

It's not really fair to label any school "good" or "bad". Schools have good years and schools have bad years and there are many complex contributory factors, perhaps the most significant among which are the home backgrounds of the individual pupils and students themselves. But there was once, in an otherwise fabulous setting, a particularly vile group of Sixth Form students who were hidden away from the rest of the college up a spiral staircase. Because they had failed to gain the requisite five GCSE passes to allow them onto 'A' Level courses, in order to stay on, they were obliged to move instead onto the (then) new GNVQ programme, resulting in quite a number of them having a chip on their shoulder and an "attitude" from the start.

I myself got off relatively lightly with them, their only real misdemeanour being the hiding of a box-file packed full of documents and records that were absolutely crucial to me on a daily basis. It could only have been students from that group who had taken it, as their room was more or less cut off from other pupils; the file's disappearance did cause me a few sleepless nights; and in despair, I referred the issue to the Head of Faculty. With her firm intervention and an amnesty established, the box-file in question magically reappeared, its contents intact; and that was the end of the matter – even if my own authority was somewhat dented in the process!

One of my female colleagues had it much worse: they would get into huge confrontations with her and deliberately wedge pins upright into the stool she was about to sit down on. Trying to get work out of most of the group was like getting blood out of a stone – and then suddenly, things took a more sinister turn...

One quiet and rather nicer-natured Sixth Former in the class came from a markedly more well-to-do background. Tall, graceful, stunningly beautiful and always impeccably dressed, she was even described as "supermodel material" by another of the Design staff. And then, one day, she began to receive threatening text messages on her mobile phone. Nobody knew who had sent them, her parents were concerned; it was a complete mystery. This was just months after the Millennium; cyber-bullying was, as yet, an unpublicised phenomenon. But what pushed things into an even more serious dimension was the discovery, just days later, of a very, very ominous letter addressed to this same girl, left on the fifth step of the studio's spiral staircase.

It was a single sheet of A4, clearly hand-written, using the tip of one of the department's own slim paintbrushes; it featured evil eyes peering out of a dark blotch, a suspiciously swastika-like symbol and red ink used to simulate dripping blood. There's a limit to the extent I can divulge here, but the girl's name was written in several places on the sheet, along with the phrase, *"R.I.P...You are being watched by my cunning eyes, to die... I have studied you and am waiting for the right time in the final stages of your life on Earth... I am coming to get you, to pounce and kill when you least expect it... Tick, tock, tick, tock, the clock is ticking."* Undoubtedly the letter was designed to generate fear, with phrases like *"I know where you live;"* and references to her family's business and location. There were also overt religious-hate and misogynistic abuse elements in what was written. The group was challenged and asked if they knew who was responsible: collectively, they denied all knowledge; but there was a distinct "atmosphere;" and I sensed a certain shiftiness among them. The death-threat letter itself ended up in the Design Faculty office where staff discussed it at length. Was it just a frivolous prank in the worst taste, or could there be a genuine intent to cause harm? At that point, the Police were brought in. I asked if I could see the letter, it was passed over to me and I studied it intently.

Now I loathe the derogatory "in" phrase "grammar Nazi" that's all the rage right now, but aside from social media (on which I enjoy relaxing and subverting the standard rules), I am an absolute stickler for correct spelling. *Instantly* – what shouted out to me were five fundamental spelling mistakes; the majority of which related to nearby regional locations peppered throughout the letter. Such was the pitifully low level of ability among that group of students, I was *certain* one of them was the perpetrator – the very use of art materials from the classroom itself indicated as much. I had just about had enough of that group: their cowardice in not owning up made me determined to uncover the guilty party and I drove home that night stewing on it; turning the problem over and over in my head.

Then it hit me: those five spelling errors were highly unusual, not the kind most people would make. The majority of us might get a single letter wrong, or double a consonant; but the chances of two students making *those* same distinct errors in each case must be remote indeed. All at once, the solution came to me: *I want to set them a spelling test!* Within which *must* be included those very same five words misspelled in the death-threat... Whoever spells them the exact same way *has* to be the culprit! And I began to devise a plan.

The test couldn't just be those words alone: the real whodunnit would be on edge anyway and would instantly pick up on it. *So the key words must be spaced out every few questions, hidden among other similar words and place names.* Let's have 20 spellings then, with one of the words dropped in, say, every five. *Yes – but these are Art students! They'll question why they're even having a spelling test! How can we go about it in such a way that they won't suspect the real agenda?* Fortunately, the highly-structured paperwork of the GNVQ course itself proved to be the solution: it was broken up into a succession of Unit Tests and Evidence Indicators. *We'll just deliver it impromptu and say this is simply a formality – another hoop they need to jump through...*

But I could never carry that off, not in a million years; they'll refuse to co-operate. *So I'll ask the Head of GNVQ, a lovely middle-aged lady, someone they already know, to bustle into the room midway through the lesson in a cheery, bubbly, everyday manner and announce she forgot to do the spelling test at the start of the course, she's really sorry, it's nothing to worry about, but we've got to get it done.* Yeah, but how do we make sure none of them cheat, look over someone else's shoulder and copy their friend's spellings? *The students will have to be called out one at a time to a separate room, with the test dictated; each word read out in order.* But if they return to the group-room afterwards, they could tell the others which words are in the test. *So they mustn't go back! Once they've done the test, they'll need to be contained somewhere separate, until all the students have been through the process... And without fail, they've each GOT to write their names at the top of their paper. Make that the very last check!*

With the devious plan formulated, I took the Head of GNVQ into my confidence the following morning; intrigued, she was only too willing to play her part. Like shooting fish in a barrel, the group didn't suspect a thing – it went as smooth as clockwork... Once the test was completed by all of them, the papers were brought to me. I literally couldn't wait... One by one, I went through the tests, ignoring the extra words I'd added as padding, but carefully checking the key spellings against the five mistakes in the letter to the girl. Thumbing towards the end of the pile, I hadn't seen anyone's results that tallied. But sure enough – the last student's crucial spellings (well – four out of five of them at least) were a *mirror* image of those same mistakes in the death-threat. I called down to College Reception. Had the Inspector come in yet? Yes, he was just entering the building. "Would you please send him down to Design immediately? I've got a result!"

A more insignificant, less likely villain you couldn't hope to imagine: the student responsible was an under-grown, bespecta-cled little Asian lad – the very *last* person in the group you would ever have expected could conjure up something so malevolent... The Police went to his home and arrested him that evening; he was flabbergasted to have been uncovered and owned up to writing the death-threat immediately; however, he remained adamant that he was coerced into the act by a much larger (and in fact, way more sinister and plausible) student in the group, who had asked the girl victim out and been rejected, and dictated the entire content of the letter to him word by word...

We never did get to the bottom of that, how true it was; to the very end, the bigger lad denied all involvement, while the smaller one claimed he had been forced to put his fingertips onto some pictures of Hindu gods and swear that the bigger student had no involvement. But certainly a question-mark hung over the pair of them from that point on. They were just weeks away from the end of their course by then; and with the college being as soft and pro-student as it was, they were let off with a five-day exclusion, a police caution and allowed to stay – by the skin of their teeth.

My part in solving the crime was far more in the pastoral domain than "educational"; but to this day, remains my proudest Teaching moment. The Inspector was chuffed as well! As he put it, "If you ever want a job in the Force, you might be good for it, mate..."

THE DOODLE GALLERY

Throughout my teaching career, I just could not *abide* Staff Meetings... I know of course they have their place and are important for conveying and exchanging information, discussing and agreeing strategies, etcetera; and that a certain maturity is required to participate, recognise and appreciate their value – but in every one, without exception (although I did my best never to show it outwardly), I would feel my spirit literally shrivelling up and dying – in fact I did my best to skive them or "forgot" to attend after school whenever I could, which I fully appreciate must have been maddening to the other department staff.

While I always gave my all, working very hard and conscientiously in any job, my attitude to meetings really highlighted a lack of inner commitment to anything long-term: the language frightened me with all the jargonised abbreviations used, which I struggled either to remember or understand; and the meetings nearly always resulted in everyone leaving with an even heavier workload than they already had. Worst of all, just when any such gathering was tantalisingly close to finally wrapping up after the best part of an hour, some well-meaning soul would niggle at a tiny, inconsequential point – and the whole thing would reignite, going on a further ten or fifteen minutes! In fairness, I suppose I may have felt differently had I ever been a more senior member of staff in charge of delivering such meetings, with a need to dispense the latest knowledge, key dates and messages; but I never was; so I just resented them.

The *only* thing which sustained me throughout the weekly ordeal was to doodle continuously using a biro; I was in fact making notes and listening actively to the points being discussed, contributing occasional viewpoints and input, so no-one ever chastised me for not focusing or told me to stop drawing; and at least doodling allowed me to create something tangible from the time I was reluctantly sacrificing. A black biro is a surprisingly versatile instrument (it's all I used, in fact, to do every illustration for this book); depending upon the weight of emphasis you place on it, you can achieve relatively subtle tonal effects, but also dramatic contrast if you require it; and, most importantly, perhaps because of the ephemeral, throwaway nature of a doodle and the fact that you're not preoccupied and precious about what you are creating, some of your best artwork can occasionally result.

I am sure any qualified interpreter would have told me that the repeated, swirling angular spirals and mazes I included conveyed more eloquently than I ever could, my inner torment and sense of being trapped; however, as well as the abstract structures, other more representational creations also emerged. Sometimes an ordinary object in view on the desktop, such as a pencil sharpener or board rubber would seize my fancy as a subject; at different times it was the speaker themselves or a colleague sitting opposite whom I drew. Other pieces were done from memory and so were more imaginative, focusing on current fascinations such as my dog, TV monsters, pop groups or other public celebrities. Sometimes I created something which I found irrationally hysterical and couldn't stop thinking about; I would have to hide it from sight and bite my lip to fight the strong urge to laugh mid-meeting, fearful of drawing negative attention to myself for demonstrating (as Judge Judy is fond of putting it) "inappropriate affect..."

The longest post I ever held was three years and one term; by the end of it, I had a 1.5 metre-long "Doodle Gallery" stuck on the wall at the side of my desk in the Design staffroom; including Croc-Face (my own fictional character), The Residents, Iggy Pop, Blondie, The Mona Lisa, Dot Cotton from *EastEnders* and her villainous son, Nick (snarling "'*Allo, Ma*" as only he could*)*, a go-ped electric scooter, my own architect's vision for a dedicated, circular hub of fruit-coloured iMacs (which we never got), treble clefs and other musical notation, Gandalf the wizard from *The Lord of the Rings*, a box of Kellogg's Special K, numerous hands, ankles and high heels visible under the desk, the goggled Crazy Frog, King Kong, an elephant and a dolphin, several door keys, caricatures of the school cleaners and Devil's Canyon from *Close Encounters of the Third Kind* – to name but a few.

The doodling antics weren't restricted to Faculty meetings either: one close colleague even used inkjet transfer paper to make some of my weekly themed GNVQ register sketches into a T-shirt for me as a leaving present; and I was staggered to discover, several years on, that the old Faculty technician still treasured one small Sontaran post-it (complete with a jingoistic speech bubble) on the wall of his own college workshop.

NARROW ESCAPE

I once had a particularly memorable Sixth Form student, who, while not of the highest ability, had such a lovely nature, a receptive, positive attitude to feedback given and a real willingness to learn – everyone got on with her and she was popular and well-adjusted among her peer group. Then – one Monday morning, she was nowhere to be seen. It was unlike her, and I simply assumed she must have come down with the latest bug and would soon be back in class. It wasn't until later that day that the Faculty received some *terrible* news... The student in question had got into a car the previous Saturday night with her boyfriend, who had been drinking. One way or another, driving at speed, he had crashed the car, which turned over; she blacked out as it spun onto its roof for the third time; but he was thrown clear, not a mark on him... she had recovered consciousness alone a few minutes later.

Somehow, the girl managed to free herself from the wreckage and stumbled several hundred yards through the darkness to the door of the nearest house – not realising the whole time that her neck was broken... She was alive, but in intensive care. The suggestion was raised that one or more of us should visit her in hospital to show support and cheer her up; but as everyone else was too busy, I volunteered, threw a giant 'Get Well Soon' card together and had all her friends and teachers sign it.

It was a pig of a night, pouring with rain as I headed into the Infirmary. I was cheery in the ward and didn't let on, of course, but to *see* that young student, previously so happy and vivacious, brought so low, was truly shocking. She was putting very much a brave face on things, able to speak and reach out, but that was about it. The student had actually been *incredibly* lucky: had the injury been more severe, she could have been left quadriplegic, unable to walk, use her hands or do anything for herself for the foreseeable future; but this was a *stable* fracture of the sixth vertebra: given her young age, and provided sufficient recuperation time was allowed, there was a high chance the bones would knit back together of their own accord and she would make a full recovery. But there was no question of her returning to school any time soon.

I happened to answer the Faculty phone a couple of weeks later, when, having come safely out of hospital, much improved, she rang into college. A highly conscientious student, she was tearful and extremely anxious about falling behind in her coursework. Most of all, she was *desperate* not to be separated from her peers and to have to retake the year among a different group. I relayed all this information to my Head of Department, offering that, if arrangements could be made, I was more than happy to go and do some home-based tuition if it helped keep the girl on track. I was struck by what seemed such an abrupt response:

"No! We *can't* have a student dictate to us how we go about things! She'll have to retake the year – that's all there is to it."

It just seemed he didn't care all that much; and I confided in a colleague, "If he had actually *seen* that girl alone: broken, silent, pale, just a shapeless blob in that white hospital bed, held rigid in a halo ring at the centre of all that apparatus – it may not be right, but I'm a human being and I – I feel emotionally involved here!"

"Of course you do," she whispered back – but nonetheless, the HoD's decision stood.

I was delighted to see that student return at the start of the next academic year to resume her Graphics course, albeit without her friends; but one day, in a quiet moment while I was working at a computer in the Faculty's open area, she came over and sat down. "Sir," she said tentatively, "you know that car accident that happened? In our culture, we have this tradition where, if you survive a near-death experience, you get a tattoo done over the injury. The tiger to us represents strength; and I wondered if you could draw me one that I can have put on the back of my neck…"

I can't remember exactly what I said! I think I spluttered some willingness to try, but as it was, my maternity cover at the college ended soon after; and the truth is, whether or not I should've done it, I could never have reconciled that lovely girl marking herself for life with any design of mine. Whether she went ahead and had something done of her own volition I'll never know – but just in case she happens to read this, to the student concerned: I never forgot – the drawing above is dedicated to you.

SITTING DUCK

As any teacher all-too-quickly becomes aware, although there is certainly a middle ground where those average pupils who are just "doing ok" are concerned, Parents' Evening tends to be a rather polarised experience, offering the best of the best and the worst of the worst. It's fantastic when you have good news on progress to report, or when delighted parents come to tell you how pleased they are with your teaching; but perhaps it's human nature that it's the cases to the *other* extreme which are the most memorable. You are really put in a position of some vulnerability; as any parent with an axe to grind knows that you are pretty much a sitting duck, there in your room to go and have a pop at if they so choose!

The singer Madonna once said something along the lines of, from 1000 people, if 999 said they loved her work – but just one person was critical, it wouldn't be *any* of the hundreds of positive endorsements that she most remembered, but that one – single – negative. And I'm rather like that too.

There was one very assertive mother who came in, not to attack me so much as to lay her firm expectations for her son's achievement on the line in no uncertain terms: she was quite intimidating, but I took solace in the fact that she had lipstick all over her teeth... And he did indeed go on to get an A* in Graphics.

Then I had this incredibly earnest dad who came to see me about his daughter. She was a very talented artist I had taught since GCSE; and she had got a grade 'A' in my subject. Unfortunately, during her continuation into 'A' Level Graphics, a degree of friction had developed between us. She would make wholly unreasonable demands, trying to bulldoze me into giving her a higher prediction on her UCAS reference than I honestly believed she would achieve; and I found her volatile, prone to sudden, really quite startling levels of rage, way out of proportion to anything I had said – her face would go white and pinched and she would quite literally be shaking with fury... The father just talked and talked and talked about my need to fully appreciate how wonderful and special she was, the impact of his separation with his wife on the girl and how I had to understand every facet of her – and when I went to get her artwork out from her shelf of the plan-chest to talk over with him, I discovered there were loads of beautiful studies of dogs she had never even shown to me! That father just would not go, or take a hint; I saw other waiting parents giving up and leaving – and he was still there talking at me at 9p.m. – when thankfully I was rescued by the welcome intervention of a senior member of staff...

Most memorable of all my visitors was a short little man and his wife who were parents to a highly academic student in my tutor group, a girl who went on to specialise in Music. The man's issue was not to do with her progress in my subject at all, as I didn't in fact teach her; it related more to her indicated level of *attendance*. The school reports, when issued, also included a record of authorised and unauthorised absences across the academic year – and I had highlighted two of the latter on her report, plus a couple of 'Late' marks. If I had made a mistake – which I very much doubt, there could have been other contributory factors anyway, as the college had just introduced these grey, laptop-like Bromcom ledgers which would 'send' the registers invisibly, via infra-red, to a central database at the click of a button. Sometimes it was announced that the system was down, and you had to revert to paper registering anyway; but once it was up and running again, you were supposed to go back and input the missed days as well as the current ones. On other occasions, if your ledger's battery happened to be running low, that could also affect the reliability of results; and it was no easy task to access them for replacement: only one amazingly versatile member of staff with thalidomide malformation of his forearm had the knack; your registers had to wait for him to be free.

So this man was sitting there, visibly seething at me; and literally quivering with ill-suppressed indignation. I took a glance over at his wife; I have never seen anyone as harried-looking as that poor woman: she looked as if she was at her wits' end, as if she'd reached her very limit: the skin around her eyes was stretched tight to the sides with a network of stress lines; I could only imagine the kind of pressure living with this man put her under on a daily basis. This was someone so driven and determined to have his own way that, even months before the sensational Total Solar Eclipse of 1999, he had booked his entire family into a hotel in St. Ives, Cornwall – the only place, supposedly, in the entire U.K. where anyone stood the slightest chance of getting a reasonable view of the event. Few saw anything of it anywhere else due to the overcast weather, but down there, at the very last possible moment, the clouds parted magically and the family had a ringside seat for the historic, once-in-a-lifetime moment of Totality...

Leaning across the desk towards me, the man took his thick, stubby index finger and jabbed it in my face aggressively, saying, "I'm not asking you: I'm *telling* you. *My* kids *aren't* late; and they *don't* have unauthorised absences. Not *my* kids. *You* are going to put that register right: I'm a Parent Governor, now see to it that you do – or *else*." He literally wanted me to rewrite history: it reminded me of Winston Smith in George Orwell's *1984*, whose job it was to 'unwrite' past newspaper articles which were in any way unsympathetic to the current regime!

I must have gulped visibly; and, satisfied that he had got to me, he stood up, took his wife and left. I think I deferred the matter to the Year Office in the end, who must have eventually "corrected" the attendance in the man's favour, as I tutored the girl for two more years and never had any more trouble from her father! But I remember running the incident past my Head of Faculty at the end of the evening, as I was more than a little shaken by the intensity of the encounter. She was a remarkable lady, so very calm and wise; and instantly responded, "This is a parent well known to us: just to put you in the picture, he has bullied and cajoled every one of his children through Oxford and Cambridge, whether or not they were suited to it: he had no right whatsoever to speak to you like that; and if anything like it ever happens again, you simply say at once, "This meeting is ended, I'm now going to bring in my Head of Faculty" – a line which I did in fact use to good effect with another stroppy parent a year or so later, who had come in to have a go at me for his son's lack of progress in Graphics.

That boy himself, while of fair ability in the subject, was a huge, burly oaf who yelled, swore and threw his weight about; and every practical lesson, whenever he was exasperated or wanted my attention, I was subject to torrents of homophobic slander, all of which I told his dad, who had no idea and couldn't believe it. "Whoa, just – hold fire one minute," he conceded, as I got up, having cited the recommended procedure I was about to follow, "Look: I know he's no angel. Let me go home and have this out with him, no way should you have to put up with that kind of thing." In seconds, he'd done a complete about-turn; and was true to his word, for at the very start of the next lesson, his son did come and murmur a contrite apology for his former conduct, going on to pass the subject with flying colours! But all this is to digress...

Going back to that previous parent, I was at home one weekend several years later around the time of the General Election, when a flyer was suddenly shoved through my letterbox. Upon unfolding it, I found it was from the extreme right-wing fascist political group, the British Nationalist Party (BNP), itself created by former members of the National Front. I ran out after the man posting them, saying, "Sorry mate, not interested in this..." – and as he turned to take it back from me, I recognised the face: it was none other than the finger-jabbing parent himself – which spoke volumes to me.

THE BIRDMAN

There is a highly multi-cultural inner-city Junior school at which I was, at one point, a fairly regular visitor as a supply teacher. The staff were all notified on a particular day that normal lessons were to be suspended for the afternoon owing to the imminent arrival of a very special guest; and that we all needed to register our classes and have them in the Hall ready by 1.30 p.m. As they were led in and sat down (an empty gangway down the centre of the room splitting the audience into two distinct halves), there were gasps of wonder from each long procession of children, all craning their necks to get a better view...

At the very front of the Hall was a middle-aged man busily adjusting the positions of a set of wooden tree-trunks of differing width, height and finish; upon the tops of which were firmly tethered the most astonishing variety of *live* birds of prey; from hawks, kestrels and falcons, to many different types of owls: a tiny, pale barn owl, a dark, brooding tawny, even some very large, foreign species – you name it – he had the lot. Now this was the rarest learning opportunity for the children: perhaps the first – and last – time they might see, face to face, the kind of winged predators you would only ordinarily get a glimpse of in the wild, view in captivity at the zoo, or watch on a televised natural history documentary. The nodding owls, in particular, were *extraordinary:* perched on each of their individual plinths like moving display pieces, their heads seemed able to rotate a full 360 degrees, making you wonder how they even stayed on the shoulders!

Clearly, this man really knew his stuff; he was passionate about his subject and spent time patiently introducing each species of bird one by one to the school: from which geographical region they originated, their dietary habits, what their unique attributes were that distinguished them from other breeds – and so on. From the youngest to the oldest, the children listened in hushed silence. When it came to the kestrel, the Birdman gave the most wonderful practical demonstration of how the breed could be trained to fly to their keeper on demand. He donned one of those large, sturdy, protective falcony safety-gloves, loosened the bird's leather jesses which tethered it to its stand and walked crisply up the gangway between the children towards the back of the Hall; as the kestrel watched him intently. Holding up a thin strip of raw meat, in one practised motion, he swung his gloved arm out horizontally. Instantly, the bird flapped up into the air, flying all the way along the aisle to land gracefully on top of the glove, claiming its reward as he secured it with the jesses – much to the awe and excitement of the audience.

Returning the kestrel safely to its plinth, the Birdman now introduced the biggest creature in his collection, an absolutely *towering* great grey Russian owl. You may think I'm embellishing the story here, but, no exaggeration – it was a monster: even from the far end of the Hall, the thing looked a good two feet high... and with its huge, penetrating eyes, its facial expression was so intense, it was scary...

"For any pupil who's confident enough to come out here and try this yourself, I'm now going to offer you the chance," said the Birdman. "Hands up if you'd like to have a go."

Well, then of course, it was an exercise in crowd-control on our part, so desperate was the sea of "Uhh! Uhh!"s and pupil arms outstretched, straining to be the lucky one chosen. In the end, it was a little girl in perhaps Year 3 or 4 whom the Birdman selected, gloving her arm up and instructing her methodically in the correct procedures, how she should stand and particularly emphasising the need for her to remain *absolutely* still once she raised her arm, as that was the signal for the owl to come.

"Now, are you ready?" he asked her gently. Unfortunately not. It was all too evident to everyone that the poor little girl had begun to have second thoughts!

So quite rightly, she was excused, went back to her space and sat down again; and the opportunity was extended once more to the eager throng. A quiet boy of around the same age was picked, the glove was put on him, and the same instructions given – but again, upon the final check, he too couldn't go through with it and backed out.

The room by this time was becoming rather unsettled; I sensed a gradual undercurrent of silliness spreading slowly, yet inexorably across the Hall.

Finally, the Birdman selected an older, rather gangling Year 5 Asian boy of around 9 or 10, who was most excited to be picked. Out he pranced into the gangway, grinning all over his face, revelling in being the centre of the whole school's attention – and, watching him, almost immediately, I had misgivings. While I hadn't actually taught that particular child, years of experience gives you an instinct, an awareness of a low attention span, poor listening skills etc – and to me, this boy seemed to tick each of those boxes. Whether I would have been listened to as a mere Supply had I tried to intervene, I'm unsure. The boy's own teacher was there, so it wasn't even my place to do so – but looking back on the day, I sincerely regret I did not voice my concerns that he appeared a less-than-ideal subject for the exercise.

I cannot fault in the slightest way how thoroughly the Birdman prepared the child for what he needed to do: the boy was gloved up, given a strip of raw meat, and warned again and again he *must* stay deathly still once he raised his arm. There may even have been safety goggles provided – I can't recall – but his understanding was certainly checked multiple times; and when he was asked if he was sure he was ready, the boy nodded and smiled by way of confirmation. With that, the Birdman left his side, walked down to the front of the room and released the giant owl from captivity on the stand. He then rejoined the boy, reiterated the instructions one last time, confirmed the child's understanding and finally ordered him to raise his gloved arm.

With terrifying speed, the owl left its perch and launched itself up the gangway, its wingspan simply *enormous*... no flapping, or flying upwards into the air like a conventional bird, this thing flew *down*, utterly *silent*, like an eerie projectile missile, shooting directly towards the boy. I'm sure it probably *was* pretty unnerving, seeing that huge, savage face looming straight towards him — it was unsettling to *me!* — and at the very last moment, just as I had sensed he might, the boy wavered, forgot the instruction — and lowered his arm...

That change to familiar procedure was *disastrous* — the owl veered to the right, lost its bearings completely and *smashed* into one of the upper glass windows near the Hall ceiling. Shaking feathers everywhere, at first frightened and then enraged, it plunged downwards, razor-sharp talons outstretched, barely inches above the mass of heads below it: a huge, real bird of prey, loose in that Hall packed with hundreds of vulnerable children. *How* none of them ended up losing an eye I will never know. As was every adult's in the room at that moment, my heart was in my mouth — I was paralysed, barely believing what I was seeing... mass hysteria throughout the Hall, the children screaming in fright — yet miraculously, none of them were attacked. The owl came down in a front corner of the Hall long enough for the Birdman to catch hold of it, regain control and return it to its stand. Then he rounded on the children, eyes blazing:

"That is the LAST time I will *EVER* come to this school! How DARE you behave like that! I *told* you you needed to stay still!" Etcetera etcetera etcetera. And that was — very swiftly — the end of his presentation. It came to an abrupt halt; the children hastily ushered out by the traumatised staff and back to their various classrooms — shaken, but unhurt.

I mean, *all* the birds there were potentially dangerous. To this day I still don't understand why anyone would select the biggest, most intimidating one by far to send towards a child! *That* was the cardinal error — a real misjudgement on his part. He probably retired soon afterwards... Given the plethora of Risk Assessments and Safeguarding in place these days, the entire visit would almost certainly never be condoned now — but then again, neither are tadpoles in the classroom (because of salmonella), frying pancakes in front of the children on a mobile stove (due to burn-risk); or appeals to parents for cardboard toilet-rolls to use in construction (for fear of spreading typhoid). All, like the Birdman, were highly educational — but these days, we live in infinitely more cautious times.

BREXIT ROUNDERS

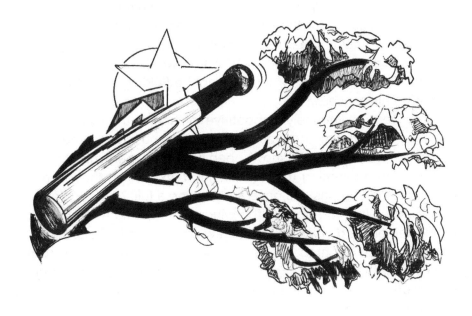

In mid-June 2016, I got a one-day assignment to cover a lively group of Year 6 pupils. Children this age are of course in their final year of Primary education; and often they start to act as if they are too cool for school. Clear, firm boundaries for acceptable behaviour need to established and they will indeed test those limits. This class was no exception – they were certainly not nasty kids, but they were none-theless big for their age, with some very strong characters among them: their energy badly needed an outlet! So to keep them on task, I dangled a 'carrot,' hinting at the chance of a major Rounders tournament that afternoon – *provided* we'd had a well-behaved, hard-working morning.

It was a gorgeous day outside and the school was blessed with lush woodland meadows. The nature of primary supply means you cover all timetabled subjects within the integrated day, not just your own specialism. While lesson plans are sometimes in place, you can't rely on them being so; and so you have to bring back-up materials of your own and be highly adaptable. Lacking any particular expertise (or confidence) in the P.E. sphere, I tended to fall back on tried-and-tested lessons. Rounders was always the one with which I had had the most success. The major topic of discussion at the time was the imminent Brexit vote, so I suggested we call it 'Brexit Rounders.' The class were quite into the ongoing political debate and the strong opinions it was generating for and against, so were very much up for this idea: we named one team "Leave" and the other, "Remain." I was rather pleased. I've really got my finger on the pulse today, I thought. The way it went, I could have been forgiven for thinking one of the lads on the fielding team had taken "leave" of his senses...

They were an intensely competitive lot; and, in the dying embers of the game, with time running out in the second innings, the scores neck-and-neck and a rain shower beginning, this particular boy was *hell-bent* on preventing the last running batsmen on the opposing team from getting past his base and scoring a full Rounder. For him, the rulebook just went out of the window altogether – he was high on excitement and an irrepressible law unto himself... Before I knew it, the boy had sprinted over to a shady tree close by; and to my disbelief, with brute strength, ripped an enormous, low-hanging bough off it. With runners in mid-circuit, he raced back to his base, oblivious to my powerful ACME Thunderer whistle and increasingly hoarse protests – wielding this *gigantic* obstacle, twigs, leaves and all – in front of him, ducking and diving back and forth to block their progress like a matador in a bullring.

Given such provocation, the game itself inevitably descended into indignant conflict between the frustrated runners and their tormentor – I think it was only the rapidly-increasing rain that defused it, enabled me to usher them back inside and save it from becoming all-out war! And perversely, considering the way that the historic vote actually went, when the scores were tallied up, our winning team that afternoon ended up being... "Remain!"

HOME VISITS

When I first began teaching 4+ classes, it was an expected part of the job to go on preliminary visits to the home of every child about to enter my class; mainly to break the ice, become more familiar and friendly to the infants and soften the enormity of their first step into full-time education; but also to touch base with the parents, allay any concerns they had and answer their questions. It wasn't a quick process: if there were 27 children in your class, that's 27 phone numbers you had to ring (assuming they were in!) and 27 different trips you went on, navigating your way to each individual house.

There were times when the entire task couldn't actually be completed within the holiday period; some of the children had already begun class by the time they were visited, but the general intention was for that initial contact to occur as early as possible. My third 4+ class was in a different school where the management were in fact rather ambivalent about the process – I went ahead and did it anyway; but by the fourth year, which was a class in the private sector, thinking had moved on and home visits were no longer the 'done' thing. The reason given for why they had fallen out of favour was because too much emphasis was being placed by certain visitors on social deprivation issues. But even so, they were incredibly interesting experiences, speaking a thousand words about the individual children and shedding invaluable light on their behaviour; and it wasn't as if you were expected to feed back either verbal or written reports about what you saw.

I personally was far more interested in the degree of parental involvement I witnessed with the children than I was in the environments. The vast majority were from Asian backgrounds; many of the parents were lovely; and incredibly supportive towards their children, spending quality time with them on various activities, from picture-books to drawing; you could see the close bond between parent and child, up at the table together working; and invariably, those were indeed the happiest and most well-adjusted children once they entered the class. I even arrived at one house to find myself revered almost as a guru: a virtual *banquet* had been laid on, with myself as guest of honour and the entire extended family gathered together, beaming, in their finest clothes around a lavish feast table, as my plate was laden with bhajis, samosas, rice and dhal – incredibly flattering but a very awkward situation to extricate myself from, as it was meant to be the briefest of drop-ins; and I had several more scheduled visits to complete at half-hourly intervals! Then, there was the home of a very unusual hearing-impaired boy which stood out only because of an absolutely *enormous* cut amethyst which stood glittering and twinkling in their hallway alcove.

I visited the home of one brilliantly artistic little boy who actually lived out of catchment area in a three-storey terrace bang in the centre of town. When I rang the doorbell, his grandfather answered the door. He looked like a frail old man, but when he shook my hand, he damn near broke it – it turned out he was a miner in his youth and was still phenomenally strong. He and the child led me up to the uppermost level of the house and opened a door – to reveal the most astonishingly-detailed model railway village I have *ever* seen – multiple motorised trains moving in opposite directions through beautifully landscaped hills, tunnels and villages, with sculpted people and working signals – quite amazing...

But then also, there were several other cases which were less-than-positive experiences. I remember arriving at one massive, freezing cold house in which the damp was pervasive; the parents were nowhere to be seen and only the little boy's older teenage brothers were in attendance; all of whom averted their gaze and just stood around silently, looking decidedly shifty. None of them seemed all that attentive or interested in the child; and worryingly, there were no toys or the usual paraphernalia of childhood visible – a total absence of stimulation of any kind, sensory, educational or otherwise. In another house, although the father was there, he was slumped in his string vest in an armchair from which he never rose, swigging from a can of beer while the kids just ran amok, tearing and screaming around us.

But the most memorable visit of all was to the house of another little boy. His mother answered the front door and invited me in, engaging me in conversation for a good five minutes – no sign of the child. After a while it started to feel a bit weird, so I asked if he was around. "Oh, yes, do go in, he's in there," she answered – pointing to another inner door which was closed.

When I opened it, the room was completely empty – all apart from the boy himself in the centre of the shiny wooden floor, dressed entirely in black, with a pile of building blocks, which he was repeatedly building up – and smashing down with all his might, then rebuilding again. We've got a right one here, I thought – and sure enough, on the very first day of school, he drove a tricycle straight at a little girl, knocking her to the ground and splitting her lip; the first of many, many misdemeanours. And his trademark action, whenever challenged for any wrong, was to expose his two front teeth over his lip – I can still picture him now...

THE POND OF EXTRA TIME

Any school or college worth its salt will usually provide a Welcome Pack for Visitors, within which you may sometimes find their own procedure for Behaviour Management (*provided* you get the precious minutes needed to actually read the thing!). As a supply, though, it really doesn't hurt to have your own individual strategies up your sleeve as well – I've seen the moistest, most inept one-trick ponies, most of whom are uncomfortable ever venturing beyond Key Stage 1, simpering: "*You're* all superstars... don't *you* want to be a superstar?" Most of the lessons such teachers deliver are about "teddies" – they don't tend to hold the attention of the average class for more than a few minutes!

I was blessed with one particular advantage, which is not only an attention-grabber, but instantly makes you appear friendly and non-threatening to any new class: I could draw. I took to those whiteboard markers like a duck to water; the only downside being that there were usually never enough colours available; so most of the artwork had to be in monochrome. But I always had a new mini-picture under my name ready to greet the children: on longer assignments, they would come through the door eager to see what each new board had to offer; and never would I let them down. The electronic smart boards have in some settings completely replaced whiteboards; and even when they've been freshly "oriented," the technology does have some way to go to keep up with a sketcher's speed. But it's usually possible to get something up on display...

Noise is one of the biggest assaults on the senses in the classroom: obviously people have differing individual limits of tolerance; and there's a certain amount of 'on-task' chat that's entirely acceptable – but for the sake of adjacent classes, especially in an open-plan environment, you do have to keep it under control. What children hate more than anything is to lose minutes of their break time, which gives you a useful point of leverage. Rather than just penalise them though, if instructions are not being listened to, it's far kinder to have a stepped warning system, so that they know when they are close to the point of no return... I came up with something called 'The Pond of Extra Time" – a big ellipse drawn on the board, with a couple of leafy bullrushes at the side. I would then add penalty tadpoles one by one. The first was "Toothy Tim," drawn with a single fang in his grinning mouth. As I added him, I would warn the class that for each tadpole that went in the pond, that was five minutes of their break gone.

On those occasions when the noise level did *not* subside, a second tadpole would go in; "Jumping Geronimo" (who was always depicted springing into the air, closely followed by a double arc of water). That was normally enough to generate collective "Shh! Shh!" noises from the children themselves to subdue their class-mates. And of course I nearly always erased the tadpoles one by one as the noise level improved. I don't think I *ever* had to add the third and final one; though I would get those children accosting me in the corridor the next day to ask what his name was:. It was the goggle-wearing, downward plummeting "Diving Demetrius", a wry in-joke: he was actually named after one of my supply agents; whose tickled response when he heard was, "I don't think I've had a tadpole named after me before!"

A CONFIDENCE KEPT

Several days a week, I used to offer after-school catchup sessions for my Graphics students. As GCSE coursework deadlines loomed, my part of the open-plan studio could become frantically packed and it would take time to ensure all the students were set up with the various equipment and advice they needed. At quieter times, though, very few, if any, would show up and I could get on with my own tasks. On one such occasion, just a single, tall, rather serious lad in glasses arrived to work on his project. He was at one of the big Formica-topped desks, while I myself was seated at the edge of the studio at a Mac, absorbed in work. He would throw over the occasional remark and I would murmur a reply; but to be honest, I wasn't paying him all that much attention. I vaguely heard him say something like, "Sir, you know when I'm at home, I don't dress like I do at college..." and I must have made some casual "uh-huh"-type response – because he continued, "No – I dress... like this..."

While still focused on my screen, something pregnant about the silence which followed eventually made me look up. There he was, standing alongside me – in a short, brightly-coloured little silk *skirt*, which he had put on over his jeans – and I could see that he was studying my expression carefully to gauge the reaction. Wrong as it may now be judged, you must understand this was around 25 years before the 'woke' LGBTQ times we have today; and I was really quite startled; however, I didn't let it show; just replied, "Oh, right..." and carried on working. But I was actually rather concerned for the student's welfare, because clearly, there was a *confessional* element, given the fact he had never dressed like that in class; and had chosen a moment when no-one else was around to reveal it to an adult.

We happened to have a College Counsellor who occupied the tiniest cubicle you have ever seen, almost like a mouse-hole in the wall, with barely room for two hard chairs facing each other; and, knowing the matter would be kept in total confidence, I decided to knock on her door the following morning and, without naming names, run the incident past her. Instantly the lady smiled and responded, "Just to let you know, I know *exactly* who you're talking about! And I can reassure you, he's one hundred percent at ease with his identity; Art teachers have a reputation for being liberal-minded, so that's probably why he chose you to approach. You might just want to ask him though in a quiet moment if he's okay with it all – see what he has to say..." Which I did, the following week. But the boy rather emotionlessly shut the topic down, claiming he had no worries or issues about it – so I dropped the subject and we never spoke of it again.

A good five years later, however, when I had long since left the college and was immersed in day-to-day supply work, I was out for lunch one day with my parents at a local Mexican restaurant. A tall figure in black came over to take our order, wrapped in a rather effeminate, frilly apron. After the waiter had gone, my dad leaned forward and, in a hushed tone, asked me, "Do you think that was a man – or a woman?" I laughed at first – but then I thought about it – and, suddenly the "skirt" incident popped back into my head; which I recounted in full to my intrigued parents. But it couldn't be him – could it? There was more than a passing resemblance actually, but that waiter wasn't wearing glasses, so I dismissed the thought. But from then onwards, for the rest of the meal, we went on to be served by a girl instead – the previous waiter *never* came out of the kitchen again...

I just had to know one way or the other, so as we were getting up to leave, I asked the girl: "That first waiter – it wasn't by any chance someone called...?" (and I gave his first name).

"Yes – that's him!" she replied. He had obviously felt too awkward to return to our table after recognising me, but still, what was nice, I thought, was that he'd found a niche in the workplace allowing him to express that facet of his character to the full.

"Please do pass on my best wishes to him!" I said – and we left.

EYE OF THE STORM

Friday afternoon! – nearly the weekend... I had been assigned, towards the very end of the academic year, to cover a lively class of Year 6 schoolchildren who had been well-occupied all-day working on their individual large-scale Transition sheets; the aims of which were to visually memorialise their best moments in Primary school and set themselves new targets for Secondary. The classroom itself was rather strange, in that, being upstairs, it protruded quite precariously from the rest of the building; almost like an add-on. While I am sure it was structurally sound, the knowledge that below it was a huge drop didn't leave you feeling exactly comfortable.

The morning had passed relatively uneventfully; with it being more a case of managing resources than lesson-teaching; and I had just welcomed the group back from lunch, completing the calling of the Register, when I happened to glance out of the window. There was a distinctly out-of-the-ordinary state of light outside; and on the playground tarmac below, I could see classes of children all dressed for P.E. running full-pelt back towards the school buildings, screaming like a spooked herd of cattle. It wasn't until I looked up that I realised why.

There, on the horizon, rapidly consuming the white sky in front of it, was the *blackest,* most oppressive *wall* of cumulonimbus storm cloud I had ever seen, advancing steadily in our direction. It was terrifying – but I said nothing to the class. It made no difference. Within seconds, like animals, they had picked up on the heightened atmosphere and began leaping from their chairs and rushing the windows, shrieking with alarm at what they saw. Their focus on work completely evaporated and I had to repeatedly order them back to their places, as rain began to hammer on the windows and ceiling; the lights flickering as thunder crashed around us.

The classroom did feel particularly exposed, jutting out like that, and these were big kids: the whole room trembled and shook every time groups of them flew to the outer edges to take another look. I had to fake anger with them for their disobedience, but how could I blame them really, with lightning flashing all around and water cascading down – it was the storm of the Millennium!

There was nowhere we could go; we were more-or-less cut off in there, as several inches of water had already built up beneath the staircase on the ground floor. To leave would have been way too dangerous, with a real risk of electrocution: it would have meant the children running across the drenched playground to access the other buildings... It was like a siege, we just had to brave it out. I imagine it must have been even worse with the younger children, but even though they were top of the school, I had to sit on this class fairly hard, as there was a real danger of it erupting into mass-hysteria; a couple of the girls were crying; and others shouting, "There's a flood – we're going to drown!" It really did sound as if the sky was splitting in two, with thunder almost instantaneous after the lightning. As I did my best to manage the frightened class and divert them into counting hundreds after each lightning-flash: "101... 102... three elephants... four elephants," etcetera, Kipling's wisdom on the virtues of keeping your head when all around you are losing theirs and blaming it on you came to mind...

Remarkably, I think we were only around a quarter of an hour late in the end reaching the pick-up point for parents at Home Time: for as quickly as it had arrived, the eye of the storm passed and the rain subsided – but what an ordeal – not just for the children either... I felt completely exhausted; wrung out – like a sopping, used dishcloth in a greasy-spoon café...

THE PETROL PAYBACK

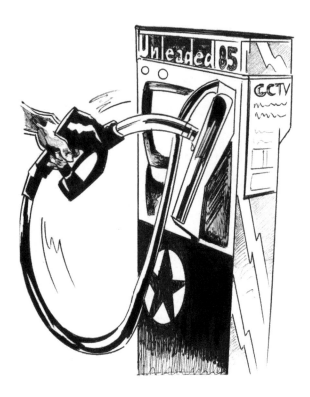

It was an evening in late summer, shortly before the new academic year was due to begin. The holiday was drawing to a close as I pulled my car into a petrol station to refuel. For some reason, at that time, I could only pay part of the bill with a debit card; the rest had to be cash; as my bank funds were low. The kiosk assistant was obstructive about this; he wouldn't give an *inch*; and made the whole exchange needlessly public so that other queuing customers heard it all.

"I don't make the rules," he went on loudly; "if you don't believe me, ring up and speak to the Manager; he'll tell you the same thing."

I will, I thought. Not only had he made a huge deal out of something very minor, he deliberately ran the entire charge through the card against my wishes, putting my balance into overdraft. The man wore one of those rectangular identity badges; so I noted his name.

When I arrived home, I rang the petrol station, asking for the Manager.

"I'm the Manager," came a familiar voice. It was *him!* – the man I had dealt with – when I asked his name, he confirmed it. So not only was he unpleasant and shouldn't have been within a hundred miles of Customer Services, he was also a liar! I rang the station's Head Office and recounted the incident. "I don't want him losing his job on my account, but he definitely needs hauling up for it," I said.

They were appalled, assured me there was no policy preventing customers from splitting a payment between cash and card; promised to have the man retrained; and sent me a £20 apology voucher. I took relish in going back to the same petrol station, filled up my car for free, walked into the kiosk and passed the voucher to the Manager. "Better have more respect for your customers!" I gloated, saying his name in full earshot of the long queue of people.

"Yes, sorry, sorry," he said, face like a beetroot as he rubbed his hands together like an obsequious bluebottle. Someone had put a major flea in his ear.

In hindsight, it probably *wasn't* my finest hour: karma's a (you know what!) and I was about to find out exactly who...

Well, the new term began the following week, and shortly afterwards, I got to meet the first of three sizeable new classes of Year 10 students – most of whom were lovely – aside from one, rather large girl... In her eyes, it seemed I couldn't do a thing right. You would think, beginning a new school, that she'd be at pains to make a good first impression – but she was one of those snide students always snickering behind her hand, rolling her eyes, grimacing and whispering into the ears of her classmates things that I could tell were derogatory, just to make them giggle. Obviously, when you begin with a brand new class that you're going to see every week for the next two years, you want things to start on a good note; to build a friendly but firm rapport with the class and have them responding well to you. I tolerated the situation for a good few lessons until I had identified a clear pattern: all the disturbances from the back table originated from this one girl – and when I checked her name against my photo-register, her distinctive surname rang a bell. *Where* had I heard that name before? It wasn't just her challenging behaviour, there was somehow a familiar *edge* to her manner that I'd encountered elsewhere... And then the penny dropped: the man in the petrol station! They had the same surname!

The next time she gave me some cheek – and to this day, I don't know why I did it – it was a true Freudian slip moment – I asked her, "Your dad doesn't by any chance work in a petrol station, does he?"

Her eyebrows shot up in amazement.

"Yeah – he does," she answered defensively. "*Why*?"

"Oh, it's just I put two and two together about something, that's all," I responded, thinking, *apple sure doesn't fall far from the tree...*

"*No*," she demanded, "Tell me. *How* do you know my dad?"

"It's nothing," I back-pedalled, "really, forget it."

But she wouldn't. I'd made it personal. On she badgered, right through Period 1, quizzing and probing and needling every time I passed her desk – until finally I'd had enough; and I said "Ok – you really want to know? Fine. He behaved dishonestly and rudely to me one day when I went to get petrol; and as a result, I made a complaint and he was disciplined."

Well, that finally shut her up – at least for the duration of the second lesson. But from *then* on, she did her utmost to make my life a living hell. Clearly, she went home and quizzed her dad about the incident, and he, upon finding out I was now her teacher, must have given her *carte blanche* to disrupt my lesson in every way possible. She would tear up paper into tiny pieces like confetti and scatter it all over the floor. The most dominant and intimidating personality in the class, over the following two years, she succeeded in turning virtually all the girls against me; even those who were initially nice and hardworking.

Most galling of all was that the group also happened to include the most gifted and talented student I ever encountered: at the age of just 14, she was a mature, accomplished illustrator: her artwork breath-taking; her compositional skill, manipulation of media: *everything* made her a flawless A* student throughout Year 10. It was she I selected from her entire year of Graphics students to do a week's placement with an award-winning, published illustrator. She should have stormed a top grade at GCSE the following year: But sadly, the gifted girl was also painfully shy; she would barely lift her head from her artwork or say a word to anyone in the lesson; and was extremely susceptible to peer pressure.

Around the start of Year 11, the other girls in the group discovered clubbing; their social lives became top priority; and I would witness the occasional mean or disparaging putdown, "swot" etc. directed from the nasty girl to the talented one; who seemed increasingly desperate not to stick out from her peers. As touches of make-up went on, down plummeted the standard of her work, along with her grades. I took her aside to discuss my concerns, asked if anything was wrong, any problems at home, etc. – but she just stood there meekly and wouldn't communicate – nothing made any difference. In the end, it was a struggle even to justify that girl a "C" in her GCSE coursework.

For any teacher to see a brilliant student fall short of fulfilling their true potential like that is the worst feeling: it leaves you with the sense that *you* – not they – have failed. But it was my strongest conviction that the other girl had been influential in destroying her inclination to focus and produce her best. I managed to hold that group together until all coursework was completed and the very final theory worksheet was handed out – there really was no more to deliver – just revision.

But then, one roasting summer's day, it was as if a deliberate conspiracy had been hatched to sabotage my lesson. The boys in the group really weren't involved; but one by one, spreading almost like a wildfire incited by that one vindictive girl, the others turned into these yammering, sibilant harpies; attacking whatever I said. I literally couldn't get a word in edgeways without a mouthful of the vilest backchat being hurled my way – and finally, after two full years of provocation from a class who had taken everything I had to give and given me virtually nothing back – I blew.

Just as sensationally demonstrated by a popular fictional, bright green, shirt-bursting colossus from 1970's tv, movies and comic-books, it's said that each of us can, at times, be possessed by an all-consuming fury. And this – truly – was my such moment.

The only way – the *only* way I can describe it, was as if my entire body in that instance, was engulfed in something *huge*: something *infinitely* larger than I was, that leapt around the outside of me. I felt 100% right and 100% justified in doing what I then went on to do. And I *really* took my time. I placed both my hands firmly on the desk, faced the class directly; and in a voice deeper and louder than I ever imagined could emanate from my own frame – one which I was later told made the very hairs stand up on the backs of the next-door PGCE student teachers' necks – I *tore* into that group.

"I am *SICK* of this class!" I bellowed... "why should I have to tolerate this *DISGUSTING* behaviour – week in, week out, lesson after lesson..." (this is very much an abridged version...) "Now I've *DONE* my job – we've completed the syllabus – any of you who won't shut up or pull your weight, don't even *THINK* of coming back – I WASH...my...*HANDS* of you. From this point forward, you are on your OWN."

There must have been shatterproof safety-glass in that door as I *smashed* it shut behind me, leaving the class in a shellshocked silence. In that moment I didn't give a damn how condemned I might be by the college for leaving them unattended – I walked out of that room and out of the building – it was what I needed to do. I went to a discreet corner where I knew I couldn't be seen, leaned against the white painted wall, soaked in the sun's rays and breathed in fresh air in peace until the bell went. By the time I re-entered the building, the class had taken their things and gone. I then consulted my Faculty Head and had the ringleader removed, permanently, from my subject. All she was permitted to do was sit the exam: predictably, she failed.

You might think from the sound of all this that I totally 'lost it'; but no. I was clear and measured, just pushed to the kind of nightmarish limit that I knew no teacher should have to tolerate – and without resorting to either swearing or assault – I defended myself. And I would do it again: they had it coming; and it was long, long overdue. Not that a meltdown such as that does you *any* physical good: within 24 hours I developed chest pains which took several days to subside – so I certainly wouldn't advocate it!

To my surprise, the rest of her class *did* attend the next lesson and the others which followed – as meek as mice. I guess they realised they'd crossed a line and that it would probably be wise to keep me on-side for their theory revision – we even went on to get some 'A'-grades; and one or two of the students stayed on to do 'A' Level. I only saw the petrol-man's daughter once more, stomping alone through the local shopping centre. She saw me; and with a face like a smacked backside, scrunched it into its habitual grimace. Then she vanished into the crowd, headed – given that attitude – for a dismal future.

EXTREME WORKAHOLISM

Workaholism is something which can creep up on you unawares, almost without you realising it... if you have things you feel you must get accomplished and no real "cut-off" to ensure you stop (such as a wife!) then you are a perfect candidate for it... Something had to give – which is why I eventually burned out, ceased working in full-time Education and moved into supply for the rest of my teaching career. I admit that much of the pressure I found myself under was self-imposed – but I just hate to let people down. And I was way, way too soft, taking on much more than one person ever should have. The worst it got was at a time when the only other Graphics teacher in the college opted to take up a pastoral Year Head's role – which left only me teaching the subject. That meant *every* Graphics student was taught by me that year. I was getting mail addressed to me labelled "Head of Graphics" when I *didn't* actually own that title! I was just a normal teacher at the chalk-face.

By and large, the students were fantastic; and the volume of Coursework they produced for their Graphics Major Project had to be seen to be believed. By the end of the year, there was a stunning A3, laminated, spiral-bound *book* from each of them; many of which had well over 100 pages meticulously logging their progress through six distinct Objectives: Design Brief, Research, Idea Generation, Product Development, Planning & Realisation and finally, Evaluation. The Coursework carried a massive 60% of their total GCSE mark, so a lot rested on it; and the deadline was made clear months before. Inevitably, though, demands from other subjects, combined with their less-than-perfect time-management skills would make the students beg for extensions; and I would do my best to accommodate them. But there would come a point when the deadline could be extended no further: the exam board itself had a specified cut-off date set in stone, by which time all projects had to be delivered safely to them with a final mark.

There were 90 Graphics students in total that year; each of whom had produced one of these massive books for me to wade through. Now you may think, why on Earth wasn't marking done on a continuous assessment basis throughout the academic year, instead of in a mad panic at the end? – and of course it *was* – at the end of each Objective – *but* the students also had the opportunity to respond to teacher feedback and improve their grades right up until the end – hence the need for that big, final mark... You had to go through each project with a fine tooth-comb, checking whether the latest targets you had set had been met; and adding those last crucial few marks wherever you could. Many of the students were a conscientious lot; and the final after-school "Twilight" sessions would be packed with them making their final tweaks, knowing that just a few improvements might make all the difference between one grade and another. I had been adamant that a particular Friday would be the *very* last opportunity for them to submit their work; I had seen to it that it was even announced in Assembly – but there were students still desperate for more time.

There simply wasn't the surface space in my own bungalow to take all these projects home, spread them out, mark them and place them all in rank order; so I had long since realised it would have to be done in college – but here we were on that Friday – and still the students weren't finished. They were really taking advantage of my goodwill; begging to take their projects home to work on for one more evening – and as a last resort, I made a final gesture to them:

"Look – I am going to be in College *this* weekend marking. You have until 12 noon tomorrow to bring me in your project: I will not accept *anything* even *one minute* after that... you'll be turned away, because I just won't have time to mark it all before it goes off to the board."

"You do realise you're a workaholic?" my worried female colleague ventured gently, when she heard what the weekend held in store for me. And I nodded. *Even* with that last extension, I still had students bringing their projects in to me at *11.59 a.m.* That left me just a day and a half to get the entire Year's Graphics Major Projects marked. I ended up bringing my Labrador Retriever, along with his food and water bowl, into College. I even had a pizza ordered from a fast-food delivery service passed to me through the window, so I could keep marking – it was the only way I could have got through the workload.

We had a gentle giant of a Premises Officer who was around 7 feet tall. I got on well with this fella – and at 9pm on the Sunday night, when I was still snowed under with work, he came to boot me out. I just had to get him on-side and explained my predicament, that looming mailing deadline first thing the next morning. I can talk about this now – as we're more than 20 years on from the event, he's long gone and no-one'll get into trouble for the security breach – but finally, he took pity on me: "You never got this from me," he said in a low, conspiratorial tone, "but here's the side door key... Leave it under the front wheel of my Land Rover when you lock up!"

With that, he left me to it. It was 3.15 a.m. on Monday morning when, shattered, I finally did so; the entire year's projects success-fully marked – and trust me, a school is an eerie place indeed to be alone in in pitch blackness! Less than five hours later, my weekend gone, I was back again to do a full day's teaching; albeit asleep at my desk at break time and through lunchtime. I just did what the job demanded.

MATERNAL INSTINCT

The toughest 4+ job I ever had in was in a village primary school in one of those pre-fab mobile classrooms, out on its own in the playground. It was *freezing* in there; and when it was icy, it seemed that there was never enough salt put down by the Premises Officer to make the steps safe – they were as slippery as a skating rink. Petrified that they were going to fall, I used to make the children go up *one at a time*, holding onto the rails – it was the only safe way – so it took ages even to get them all inside: I barely had time to register them before assembly! There were 31 tiny children which was tough enough – then one day, the Head dropped a 32nd on me – just like that – with a message relayed via T.A: "You've *won* her."

Forget the problems integrating the child and doing her Baseline Assessment in an already-established, busy class – I could have sworn she was *two* – masquerading as a four year-old. She had zero focus and you couldn't reason with her in her little dungarees – turn your back for half a second and she'd be out the door.

Another sad, malnourished-looking child in the same class wasn't properly toilet-trained and had pre-diagnosed issues with his digestive system: one day, while I was busy hearing another child read, I heard this agitated wailing rising into a frenzy; and looked up to see the traumatised boy lunging at me like the gas-exposed soldier in Wilfred Owen's *Dulce Et Decorum Est*, hands covered in diarrhoea – I have never leapt out of a chair so fast... He went home sick and didn't return – just wasn't ready for school.

And then there was a tragic case of a little boy who'd got hold of his mother's cigarette lighter while she was asleep and burned their house down. His little sister died in the fire and he required extensive skin grafts on his hands. The mother would send him to school without mittens in sub-zero temperatures – he would be crying with the pain and cold – and there she would stand, still smoking. I would end up having to spend my own money to buy the children crayons and felt-tips, because the Headteacher refused to provide them; she wouldn't even allow me use of the photocopier. I had to use this monstrous, antique Banda, which used outsize paper that had to be fixed on the drum and was turned manually by a handle to make copies. The ink was purple and smelled like pear drops – you almost got high on the fumes...

In some ways the school was unusual. It had a long, heated swimming pool built into the side of a corridor; and all the children could swim with floats from the age of five. But it wasn't a job I stayed in long, such was the level of stress and lack of support from the Head – she was a petite, but foul-tempered, absolute autocrat who would enter my classroom unheralded and remain, looking over my shoulder, intimidating and correcting me all day. Writing an open letter to the Chairman of the Board of Governors and the parents of every child in the class to say how much I loved the children, but that circumstances at the school had made it impossible for me to continue, I resigned, claiming constructive dismissal. There was an absolute outcry on my behalf from the parents, the Head left soon after and I had to be replaced by not one, but *two* teachers, such was the workload in that class.

None of these elements however, were the most potent memory of that time. There was one particular moment which seared itself into my brain... It was Home Time, and I had safely delivered all the children back to their respective parents, one of whom decided to stay and have a natter with another mum in the playground – which was nothing uncommon. In so doing, either she took her eye off her little girl (who was an only child); or the child managed to slip her hand – one or the other – because around 20 minutes later, while I was engrossed in marking, the outer door to the mobile classroom opened – and in came the little girl on her own! Thank goodness she had the sense – at just five years old – to do that. I was surprised and asked her what she was doing back, where was her mum, etcetera – but she sucked her thumb nervously and didn't say anything. I couldn't see anyone left in the playground, so the safest thing was to walk the little girl all the way up to Reception in the main building and leave her securely with the other late pickups who were supervised by the office staff.

Returning to the mobile to resume my marking, I had barely sat down again when the door literally *burst* open – and in fell this little girl's mum, *hysterical* with fear, tears pouring down her cheeks: "My baby! My baby's gone, my baby girl..." – I have *never* seen anyone in such a state of raw, primal terror; in her panic, she couldn't even hear me assuring her that her child was ok. In the end, I had to take the poor lady by the shoulders and *shake* her: "She's *alright,* I promise...She came back to the classroom and she's safe in the Office." The relief on that mum's face... she just couldn't stop saying: "Oh Thank you – thank you, thank you – thank you soOo much" and the tears continued, but now they were positive, happy tears of exhausted relief... To that point, responsibility-wise, I had probably been coasting through my Teaching years in something of a daze – but that experience really brought home to me, more potently than any other, just how *infinitely* precious are each of those tiny little charges we have in our care – and how catastrophic it would ever be to become complacent and allow a disaster to happen to even one of them on our watch.

CIRCLE TIME

Circle Time on the carpet with the tiny ones is generally a more relaxed part of the morning, when the children can have a short story before break, drink their milk and take a fruit from the basket. It is also a good opportunity to instil positive social skills. I *loved* it, looking strict and feigning a stern tone when in fact I was laughing inside...

"Uh-uh – *NO* – the one you touch is the one you *TAKE!* And *what* do you say?"

"Thank you."

"That's better."

They loved it all too. Even the gentle scolding – I know they did. It was such fun for us all – like a daily picnic indoors. Sometimes I would put on music; their favourite by far was *The Laughing Policeman* by Charles Penrose. They studied *everything* I did, absorbing it like

85

sponges. Parents would tell me that on clothes-shopping trips, their children would say "I want clothes like Mr Guy."

Knowing the impression I made would sometimes make me mischievous. I would look at them with a deadly serious expression and say, "You've got to be grown-up when you're drinking. Do you want to know what cowboys say?"

I would put on an exaggerated Wild West drawl and holler: "*GIT off Yo' hoss and drink Yer milk!*" – then, "Everyone say it."

And with delight, all the little Asian children would clutch their milk bottles tight and shout, "*GIT OFF YO' HOSS AND DRINK YER MILK!*"

Well of course, this little nugget would come back to them once they were at home. I would hear the following day from one or more sets of parents that at dinner-time, their little infant had had the entire family in hysterics!

Not all days were such a pleasure, however...

"Hold it with *BOTH* hands!" I would command, all too aware that the lingering smell of milk spilled into a carpet is enough to make a whole class nauseous for weeks... Suddenly, no sooner had he finished his bottle, than this small boy began to cough and splutter... A warning, the rest of this tale makes for difficult reading, but... one had the impression that droplets of milk were coming from *every* orifice: his nose, his ears and mouth – and then suddenly – blurrrrgh! he threw up an *unimaginable* amount onto the carpet – it must have curdled the moment it hit his stomach...

Instead of being upset, he was fascinated and began putting his fingers in the mess and drawing it upwards. Worst of all was that the other 4-5 year-olds were also interested in investigating and it was all we could do to keep them away from it! I felt such a "teacher" getting the classroom assistant to put the standard pile of sawdust, Ajax, Vim or whatever it was fizzing away on top of it all – and then, the obligatory *chair*...of course, the little boy had to be sent home in case he was infectious; however, we were not out of the woods yet...

Later that afternoon, with the Premises officer having failed to arrive promptly, we spotted that one or more children had practised their letter formation in the vomit; and had to send them all to the toilet again to wash their hands with soap and hot water! Ah – the joy...

THE CHARM OFFENSIVE

Headteachers must surely talk among themselves when they meet at this or that function; for towards the end of my very first temporary Infant school job, I was notified that the Head of another nearby school wished to see me. I was riding high on confidence at that point, as the current class had gone very well; I had more or less been given my head to run things as I saw fit, with virtually zero paperwork aside from reports; and very little pressure from on high to do anything in any particular way. So I felt there could be no harm in accepting the invitation to this other school, if only to see what it was like and find out why I had been asked.

I have never known a day like it. The Head of the neighbouring school had arranged for another of her teachers, some vague ex-college acquaintance of mine (who in truth, I never really knew all that well!) to meet me at the front entrance: she flung her arms around me and embraced me joyfully as if we had been lifelong, long-lost friends; she took me for a walk around the block and told me all her deepest, innermost secrets; then I was ushered into the Head's office like royalty. It was coffee and biscuits and welcomes all round; the governors were hanging on my every word, compliments galore – and by the end of the day, my jaw ached from all the smiling required as I was introduced to this person and that – I couldn't say a thing wrong. Finally, the Head came down to business: she was looking for a teacher to cover the same 4+ age for the following academic year: might I be interested?

It's fair to say I was 100% *flattered* into accepting the job. Let that be a lesson to you. Had I been a little more astute I might have picked up on the less-than-sincere body language; questioned perhaps the motive behind all those ingratiating smiles and the over-effusive welcome. But I didn't. I accepted there and then; and arrangements were made for me to come in the following Tuesday to meet the staff and parents after school.

The atmosphere on that day could not have been any more marked in contrast. Gone were the encouraging smiles and gushing welcome: it was a very lukewarm reception now – no-nonsense talk about all that the job would entail; the parents seemed entirely disinterested and the Deputy Head was particularly cool and unfriendly, her manner making it clear in no uncertain terms that my appointment was not one she approved of. It seemed she was trying to pinpoint some area of weakness in me that might be ripe for attack...

"You've changed your name, haven't you? You have – I can tell you have..." was the first thing she said. I had barely opened my mouth to respond and, "You're sensitive about it, I can tell!" came her next remark.

It was no big deal to me that I chose to work under an 'alias,' but the way she put it was as if there was some deep, dark secret involved that I wanted to hide! I was given this horrid, heavy school dinner, followed by a stodgy spotted dick pudding in gloopy yellow custard; and looking across the table I felt I had nothing in common with the other staff; it was as if they were another species... In particular, it was brought home to me by the Deputy Head how crucial it was that I must follow the then relatively new National Curriculum to the letter. A four foot tall trolley on wheels was brought to me, upon which were dumped some 30 full files of government-dictated statutory and non-statutory guidance I would need to adhere to. It was clear the aim was to swamp me – and it worked. The difference between the freedom I had had in my current job and this highly-prescriptive approach made my head spin – I took all the material home – but the truth was, that as I waded through it all, I just didn't know where to begin. I now had a thoroughly bad vibe about the job and the staff. *What* had I committed myself to?

Experience has taught me over the years that you *must* listen to your inner voice; and mine was telling me very loudly indeed that I had made an error of judgment here. I rang my own Head before school the next morning and confessed all my misgivings.

"I don't know – all you arty types!" she exclaimed in mock-exasperation. "Well, you'd better go back straight away and face the music, hadn't you?"

I knew she was right; the sooner the better. Given the morning off, I returned to the other school and waited in trepidation outside the Head's office. Along passed the teacher who knew me from college. Seeing my hangdog expression and the trolley of returned National Curriculum folders alongside me, she put two and two together in an instant: "You've had second thoughts, haven't you?"

I nodded guiltily.

"I don't blame you," she said. "To tell you the truth, I think you've had a lucky escape. It serves her right: she's a bloody nightmare to work for; she's had several teachers resign this year!"

So now I knew why I had been sought. The door to the Head's office finally opened.

"Come in," she said briskly. "What's all this about, Guy?"

I had to come straight out with it.

"I – I don't know how to say this," I stammered, "I'm really sorry but I've changed my mind about the job."

Whereupon the Head flew into a rage: her face purple with fury. "Someone's *got* to you, haven't they? Who is it? You tell me!" (She wasn't entirely wrong there, but I wasn't about to name names). "Do you know I've got a stomach ulcer playing up from all the stress I'm under? I don't need this as well!" she shrieked. "Get out of here. I never want to see your face again!"

Having shown her true colours, I was now *certain* I had made the right decision. The worst was over; and I felt freed from a heavy burden as I returned to my car. A momentary deviation, but now I had corrected course. It turned out to be the right thing to do. I took a term off, then was reinstated in the same familiar school for a second two-term maternity cover. My only real concern about the episode was that we had all been warned in no uncertain terms at Teacher Training college that it was a cardinal sin to accept any job, then change one's mind; something that could lead to "blacklisting." I really was very worried for a while that, should that Head decide to be vindictive, she might well have me named and shamed. But, as the years have gone on to prove, no such blacklist ever really existed: the real moral of the story is not to be so easily taken in by flattery but to look a little deeper; and listen carefully to that guiding voice inside yourself: it will seldom let you down.

THE LONG-TERM SICKNESS COVER

In one large local college, I was a regular visitor as a supply teacher. It had arguably the worst behaviour of any of the schools I visited. In the days before it got demolished and reconstructed into a flash new state-of-the-art building, classes were split between two different sites, with five minutes' movement factored into the timetable between lessons; which the pupils would exploit endlessly, blaming their late arrivals at your room on the timing of the bell in the other half! There were also a fair amount of violent altercations. I once saw a fight erupt between two pupils which spilled into the actual School Office. One of them was a new boy who had been "buddied" up with an existing pupil; the latter of whom had seized a powerful dislike to his new charge. I have no idea what exactly had happened between the pair of them, but the regular pupil had warned staff that should he as much as see the other lad, he would beat him up. This new boy was so frightened by the prospect that he asked me to escort him across the playground. His fears proved to be absolutely justified as the other boy was lying in wait for him and sprang out suddenly at us from behind a wall, launching into the newcomer with unbridled savagery.

The recommended strategy now is that you do *not* any longer wade in between the parties and try to "break it up" (although, at least at Primary level, instinct for the preservation of the pupils involved led me to do just that on more than one occasion!) – you are instead meant to isolate the fighters from others around them. The two of them were beating the hell out of each other and it escalated into the very midst of the pool of secretaries; one of whom famously suffered so badly from stress that pressure would build up behind her eyeball to the extent that on one occasion it actually popped *out* of her head into her hand, still attached by the optic nerve! Fortunately, a nearby doctor from the practice next door gently eased it back into the socket...

On one of my first mornings there, I had a late call and arrived to find the car park jammed full; in my haste not to be any more late entering the building, I resorted to parking my old Saab, a bit of a rust-bucket by then, on the grass verge. Big mistake: by the end of the day, the wheels had sunk into the ground. What I couldn't see, as I revved the engine in reverse to free the car, was that the back wheels were spraying a jet of pressurised mud all over the cars behind me – out ran the agitated office staff shrieking in concern, having spotted the disaster on the CCTV – as you can imagine, I was most popular with the owners of the vehicles behind me after that! Such was the force of the revving that the mud also found its way up inside my rear axles and even the disused boot; so that when the car's M.O.T. came up a few weeks later, it was instantly condemned as "beyond economic repair" by our family's time-served mechanic. "I've never seen anything like it – it looks like it's been driven around on a bloody farm!" he exclaimed incredulously as I feigned bewildered innocence...

There was however, one blessing in the midst of this highly challenging environment: The Design department was filled with the most wonderful, very different, yet spirited group of staff. From the humblest technician, who daily unwrapped and laid out his packed lunch from a serviette with all the dignity and grace one might apply to a royal banquet, to the Head of Faculty, they just gelled together so well... I'm not saying there weren't creative tensions, because there could be, but they welcomed me as a kindred spirit, even after a time introducing me to others as "a friend of the Faculty" – and they put up an absolutely united front in their stance towards pupil behaviour. Even on those occasions when I was doing General Cover in other parts of the building, I would head for the haven of Design at lunchtime.

Among them was the most angelic looking, elfin-faced young Food teacher who I just clicked with from day one: she had sold on a successful restaurant she had created from scratch to go into Teaching: how dedicated is that? – yet she had been treated really thoughtlessly by the school's senior management. As an unqualified, though highly talented teacher learning on the job, they had given her possibly the toughest, most unsettled Year 7 tutor-group in the college. It seemed that the general aim was to drop that teacher in the deep end to discover whether she might sink or swim; all of which she took in her stride – although I know the group brought her to the point of despair on more than one occasion.

Now it was tradition year-on-year in this Faculty to have a 'sweep-stakes' whenever *I'm A Celebrity: Get Me Out Of Here!* was back on TV: each of us would put a couple of pounds into the kitty, get assigned one of that year's jungle celebrities via a random process; and 12 or so weeks later, the full amount would be claimed by the holder of whichever famous name won the process – if that makes sense. It wasn't my first encounter with this show in a school envi-ronment: another primary school I often visited had held a spoof *I'm a Teacher: Get Me Out Of Here!* assembly a year or so before, in which the notoriously practical-joking Head got carried away. While I was bent forward under a cloth retrieving bobbing apples with my teeth from a bowl of water, he brandished a full bottle of vegetable oil behind me so that the audience could see its full horror, then poured the entire contents down the back of my T-shirt in front of the whole, cringing, school... They were right to cringe: the sensation was pretty vile – and despite the grateful receipt of a couple of towels, I had the rest of the day's sticky teaching to endure: the things one did for charity!

But anyway, back to the Secondary school. I hadn't worked there for some time, having been engaged in more Primary assignments, when one day, a booking came in for that college to cover a sickness in the Design department, its duration uncertain. Among the staff in the Faculty was a deeply religious Hindu Art and Ceramics teacher; a very kind, gentle little man whose lessons I had sometimes covered. He was way too soft for those tough kids, however; and they took merciless advantage of him. There are of course two sides to every story; but the way it was relayed to me by the other staff was that this particular Asian staff member had won that year's *I'm a Celebrity* sweepstakes fund. Most people had paid him what they owed him immediately; however a number of teachers had failed to do so. A couple of weeks later, he had reminded them for a second time that they owed him his winnings; and when they still failed to pay up, whether you judge it right or wrong, over-reaction or otherwise – he reportedly "played the race card" – made a complaint and claimed the non-payment was down to racist discrimination.

So aggrieved at this accusation was one of his white women colleagues (who had already had friction with him over a number of other issues) that she invoked the involvement of one of her close friends, who happened to be the Deputy; that person came and observed the man's teaching and immediately placed him in "formal capability proceedings" – meaning that she was present in his lesson scrutinising every aspect of his teaching, both paper-based and practical, from that point forth. After week upon week of this onslaught, plus piles of extra admin she loaded onto his shoulders, the poor man came home one night and collapsed in front of his family. Whichever side people took, the whole thing was ridiculous: a storm in a teacup which had been blown way out of proportion: the school now had to pay me for weeks to cover his sickness.

In the meantime, the man's classes had run absolutely amok: on the desk, I found a religious tassel of his tied-off hair which one of the more challenging pupils had chopped off with a pair of scissors, having tiptoed up behind him on his final day; another boy had made a large set of male genitalia out of clay and left it out on the man's desk: this the Head of Faculty took great delight in photo-graphing to show the boy's parents what their son was getting up to in school! On the front of the classroom door had been posted the word "bhenchod" – an Indian and Pakistani obscenity I will leave to you to look up if you so choose – a Year 7 boy was making a huge pool of spit on the desktop, dipping classroom pencils in it and then throwing them onto the floor... anyway, you get the general gist of the situation I was taking over.

It really did take a week or two for the penny to drop to those pupils that I was no pushover and was here for some time to get them under some semblance of control! They were studying the lively artwork of the recent Turner Prize winner, Chris Offili, whose colourful pictures famously made use of elephant dung; another project centred on the Mexican Day of the Dead festival complete with sugar skulls and sweet-filled piñatas; so there was no shortage of ongoing work to keep them occupied. But on one circuit of the classroom, I suddenly felt a stabbing pain in my right middle finger: to this day I firmly believe one of them actually *shot* me with something concealed under desk-level: not anything that physically penetrated, you understand, but possibly a taser device or something generating a massive, localised electric shock – I have no idea. At first I thought it was broken: that finger, before my eyes, swelled to *double* its normal width – I was quite literally in agony – but no way was I going to give that class the satisfaction of knowing they had got to me. Hoping to gather more evidence of the weapon used and the attacker, I said nothing; however I never did get to the bottom of it. The finger took a good hour or so to subside to its normal size; and the incident remains a mystery to this day.

The most chilling aspect of all about the cover though had to be the presence, in one Year 9 class, of a girl who was strongly suspected by the 1:1 support staff to be a "sexualised child" – she was meant to have the most *awful* home circumstances... Only once had I ever encountered that dreadful phenomenon before, in America; it's not until you teach such an unfortunate pupil yourself that you can fully comprehend how frightening they are... They are somehow *not* children at all: there is an inappropriate directness; an adult awareness they have been made to possess prematurely, way beyond their years – this girl would only ever refer to me as "Mr Willy" – it seemed her entire focus and agenda was on a suggestive, sexual level – all her communication sought to make a connection of the wrong kind: she gave me the absolute creeps and to be honest, I did my best to keep my distance from her as far as was humanly possible in that classroom. And thank goodness for the presence of other adults!

I was at the college one day short of 12 weeks, after which they would have had to pay me Teacher's Pay Scale: I, however, would then also have been expected to take on the full marking, admin and report-writing workload of a regular member of staff – all the things I had gone into Supply to be freed from – so I was only too happy to go. I felt so sorry for the way that man had been treated who was driven off sick that I obtained his contact details from one of the other staff and took him to the cinema for an evening – just to get him out. He was at a very low ebb indeed; as if things weren't bad enough, his wife had left him – and he never did in fact return to his job: at first he was on full pay, then half, then quarter pay; then the college informed him they had taken legal advice; he either left with a fair reference or came back – and he chose not to. Last thing I heard, he had gone to London to begin a new life; and to be 100% honest, I don't really blame him.

THE ELECTIVE MUTE

Although an outdated term, elective mutism defines the refusal to speak in almost all social circumstances (despite the ability to do so). Another condition, *selective* mutism, indicates a failure to speak in just *specific* situations, something which is strongly associated with social anxiety disorder. Only once ever did I encounter the phenomenon – in a female Foundation 2 pupil. In some respects, the mutism made her very powerful indeed, not only as an object of curiosity among her peers (some of whom would protect her like a pet, dressing her up (which she very much enjoyed) in the various play costumes and presenting her to me for approval); but also because, if a child refuses to answer their teacher, there is a limit to what the teacher can do to ensure their participation in certain activities

– which in turn makes it look as if they are succeeding in defiance and leads to some of the others jumping on the bandwagon and trying on similar behaviour!

My own opinion was that this infant was most definitely a "selective" mute rather than the "elective" one she had been labelled; but this was a 1995 class; the term "selective" had only been adopted in 1994; so may not have permeated through to general use by then. Most certainly the girl could – and did – speak at home; her parents even brought in a tape-recording of her doing so, giggling and saying her own name whilst engaged in play. The theory is that children with selective mutism are not *choosing* to be silent (as the term "elective" implies), but are just too afraid to speak in a setting in which they are expected to, such as school; despite speaking readily in other situations. One thing the girl *would* do, is use one or more of the other girls as mediators: to them she would speak; and they would come and tell me what she had said, or asked for. I can rule out that it was me, specifically, she was scared of; we actually had a good rapport, she would point readily to a correct picture when asked and had already come to me with that diagnosis since Nursery.

It was usually very clear if any child was scared of me: one little girl in the same class who joined the school without having been through Nursery was so terrified on her first day that she clung desperately to her mother's sari until physically disengaged from it by a Teaching Assistant. She then went Into a frenzied tantrum in the cloakroom; a mass of pummelling fists and feet – in her panic kicking me in the face... We plonked her down with the coats and packed lunch-boxes and left her to get it all out of her system; after 20 minutes, her screaming subsided to crying; after a further 10, she was quietly led in to join the rest of the children – and she never gave us any trouble again!

In the mute's case, I did spot one particularly odd thing: at Home Time, the vast majority of collecting parents would greet their children with joy once the outer classroom door was opened. They would smother them in hugs and kisses or swing them into the air – but in this child's case, there didn't appear to be the same degree of warmth. The father would come into the building from a different direction via the main entrance. He would make his way through to our open-plan area and merely call to the girl, or sometimes make no more than the briefest eye-contact from some 50 yards away;

then turn on his heel and walk out – and the little girl would toddle after him – way behind.

I tried every strategy I could to make her speak, talking down a cardboard tube to alter my voice, not looking directly at her when asking a question; whatever I could think of – but nothing worked. A month or so in, I realised that a large number of the children in the class were unable to say the word "crisps" correctly – they would say "crips" – and, via an amusing discussion, we agreed at Circle Time to conduct a proper class survey to find out who said what – and present the results as a bar chart in Assembly. It was very close, about half-and-half – but of course, when it came to the mute girl, she didn't say *anything* – I had to say that she had chosen to "abstain" from the vote – but I'd bet my life she would have said the word correctly; she was so bright...

That summer we had a school trip to Elvaston Castle Country Park in Derbyshire. Those were the days of the home video-camera craze; and with a fantastic ratio of staff-to-pupil support, I was able to bring a camcorder to film every aspect of the trip. For the end of the video, each child took it in turns to climb up into a hay-filled cart; wave and shout out their name for their proud parents; but as expected, when it came to the mute girl's time to go up, she remained silent. I didn't want her to stick out in the film for that; fortunately, I still had that home recording the parents had given me of her saying her own name; and I managed to dub her voice over the silent footage; much to the girl's surprise when the class watched the video. It sounds wrong to use the word "dumbfounded" in this context – but clearly that's what she was!

On the very last day of term, it came to be her turn to read to me again. Bear in mind this was a child who had failed to say a single word in three months, while all the others were learning phonics, recognising more and more vocabulary and progressing steadily through the reading scheme. I called her over gently, she stood at my side, I pointed to each word, and all of a sudden, I heard a strange little voice: "*Vun, two, t'ree...*" In that single session, she read three consecutive books – flawlessly – not a single mistake. I was overjoyed. *Breakthrough*, I thought – and made a big fuss of her in front of the class: children and adults alike all gave her a huge round of applause – it was a special moment.

In teacher training, however, you are taught to be a "reflective practitioner" – and in hindsight, making it a big deal, I think, was a mistake. If I hadn't made such a thing of her starting to speak, hadn't even remarked on it, maybe it would have normalised her doing so. But some external factor, I feel sure, was also involved. That little girl went away for the Easter holidays, came back – and *never* spoke again; not just in Reception, but for the next *six years* – the rest of her Primary school days. The educational psychologist was involved; staff were worried that if she entered the Secondary sector still mute, the die would be cast: so socially disadvantaged would she become that she may be stigmatised forever, preventing her from living a normal life. But amazingly, as if a magic spell was broken, the start of Secondary was also the point when the girl *did* begin speaking; judging from the way it was reported to me, she was fine from that day forth...

SHOWMANSHIP AND THE MYSTERY MANTRA

Whenever I had something exciting or unusual to show children of any age, I would create a sense of drama: build up to the big reveal, rather than just present it outright – you are something of a showman anyway as a teacher... A bag is, of course, a great device. The kids are always seething either to reach themselves into its darkness or be shown what is inside and watch it being lifted out; but the usual hand behind your back comes a close second. I can't just get them to say "Abracadabra," I thought. That's a cop-out – I can do better than that... So I came up with this made-up triple-phrase; and when I had something to show them, I would get them to say each word after me:

"Avashna…"

"AVASHNA…"

"Ashindi…"

"ASHINDI…"

"Ishabola!"

"ISHABOLA!"

– then, with a powerful stare, I would bring out the mystery item.

"WhoOa!" they would say, or (in a "bad-is-good" spirit, which I hated), "*Sick!*"

The children loved that routine – and I used it for years, thinking it was just nonsense I'd conjured up from thin air. But one day, something made me dwell on those words and become curious about them – they had seemed to come out of nowhere – *where* did I dream them up from; and what in fact might I be saying? I decided to look the three words up individually – and I couldn't believe what I discovered…

"Avashna" is one of the eight petals of the divine lotus flower in Buddhist mantras and mandalas, "Ashindi" is a name frequently used in Hinduism; and most astonishing of all, "Ishabola" is an African Bemba word meaning… "The Voice of Prophecy."

It turned out I wasn't talking gobbledegook at all: I was more-or-less speaking in tongues…

WEAPONS OF MASS DISRUPTION

Although I did the odd day of supply here and there as far back as the mid 1990's, it didn't become my main job of work until 2003; coinciding rather strangely with the start of the Second Gulf War... A well-known local community college was my first assignment: they were great, as you were booked for a full week at a time; so I ended up with around six weeks' solid work there, which was pretty rare. It was General Cover; but the vast majority of it was to replace a member of staff on long-term sick-leave from Humanities. That wasn't my subject, but if you were a good all-rounder, with any degree of competence, you could fairly quickly get your head around the tasks.

Most of the lessons involved the pupils reading a double-page of textbook material and then answering a set of comprehension questions on it – a process I was more than familiar with when teaching English. This was a good, well-run situation in which you didn't have to mark; and the work for the day was always sellotaped to the desk, so you knew exactly what had to be delivered to each class.

The Year 7 and 8 groups were no problem at all – but the Year 9's were *horrid*... They were just at the age when they shot up in size and height; and there were some massive lads in that group, way bigger than I was, who clearly enjoyed throwing their weight about: with skyrocketing levels of testosterone, they could be quite disrespectful towards certain of the female students in the group. It was one of those classrooms with a very dated triple chalkboard on a vertical loop; you could pull down the next board when the one you were writing on got full. But chalk wasn't the easiest or fastest thing for me to use; and obviously some students were quicker than others at getting through the questions and needing the next board, causing friction between the slower and faster ones. "Hey wai-*wait*, Sir – *SIR!* – I've not finished! Bring it back, Sir!" – and, of course, there was the inevitable temptation for them to pelt things at each other when, out of necessity only, my back was turned; either to pull the next board down or to write extension tasks for them.

So the behaviour was unsettled – at best – when suddenly, the door to the classroom was *kicked* violently open – and this *huge* lad with a box-style fabric hat on his head burst in (no apology for being late), face lit up with missionary zeal, shouting, "SADDAM HUSSEIN'S JUST LAUNCHED A NUCLEAR MISSILE AT THE UK – WE'RE ALL GOING TO *DIE!*"

The class *erupted* into chaos... I got the distinct feeling there was more than a small element of enjoyment there at both disrupting education in the West and spreading fear – one of the Asian girl students promptly burst into tears – so I had two things to deal with simultaneously: not just the boy's behaviour but also calming this poor girl down.

"*YOU* can have a Sanction slip for that," I said, raising my voice, "and as for any weapon launch – *one* -it's not true (I had to fake confidence there; the news of an attack on us *could* have just come in for all I knew; as the UN Inspectors' search for Iraq's Weapons of Mass Destruction was ongoing at the time!) – and *two*, if there was such an attack, don't you think our missile defence system would blast it out of the sky before it even got here?"

At least that stopped the poor, frightened girl crying. The end of that lesson and morning break couldn't come soon enough; it was like a herd of water buffalo or wildebeest leaving the room as they shoved and tumbled out – and on his way past, the same lad deliberately kicked over the dark-green metal waste bin; sending scrunched up, ink-stained balls of paper and other debris flying across the room as he exited, laughing.

I yanked the classroom door open; there was only one way out for the students – down the staircase – and I spotted him on the mezzanine floor below, almost obscured by continuing downward traffic from the level above. Throwing caution to the wind, I roared, "I *FORBID* YOU TO GO DOWN THOSE STAIRS! *GET* BACK UP HERE!"

At least at that point, my voice must have held sufficient authority, for he did, sheepishly, return, in full view of those passing by – and, still quivering from the outburst, I stood over that student as he got down on his hands and knees and picked up *every* last vestige of chocolate wrapper, crisp packets and paper. Then I wrote out a detention slip for him and sent him on his way – having missed most of his break. The exasperating thing was that you could follow the school's behaviour policy to the letter, posting the requisite slips into the required box on a Monday – but the box wouldn't actually be opened and dealt with until the following Friday – by which time you had often taught the student involved *again*, their conduct unchanged – as no-one had addressed the matter!

But the stance of Senior Management was that the feedback was still of value, as it helped to build a broader picture of that student and their behaviour across a longer period of time. You have to have a lot of humility and anger management skills to be a supply teacher – and sometimes, frankly, those you teach can – and do – get the better of you! Gotta take the rough with the smooth though – or don't do it...

THE CRUSH

I was relaxing one break time, drinking coffee in the staffroom of a primary school I visited frequently, when in walked the Deputy Head, paused at my chair, leaned over and asked confidentially, "Do you mind if I have a word?" I followed her down the corridor to her classroom with a growing feeling of trepidation, thinking, here we go; what have I done wrong? – but once her door was sufficiently closed to afford a level of privacy, she said, "This is very awkward, but... look, there's someone here who *really* likes you... she's taken me into her confidence; and I've promised her I would speak to you about it."

I must have been speechless for a moment; for she was quick to follow that with the words, "Oh, she's *not* staff..."

"Not staff?" I echoed. "Who is it then, a parent? Oh no – it's not a pupil is it..."

"No, no," she continued, "she's a Lunchtime Supervisor." ("Dinner lady" we used to call them).

I began spluttering in embarrassment: "It's just... I'm *really*, really choosy, infinitely more so than I have a right to be... but I, I just can't stand hurting people... who is it?"

She gave me the woman's name – but I was none the wiser.

"Well, what does she look like?" I quizzed her.

"Well, she's got one of those... grey partings," she said, and left it at that, as the bell was ringing to signify the end of break.

Given that description, I was already having misgivings; and after asking discreetly around, I was pointed in the woman's direction, only to spot a lady in a long, black, buttoned coat down to her ankles out in the playground; someone I'd said a passing, friendly hello to a couple of times, but that was all... Clearly she'd seized a liking to me; but "grey parting"? That was the diplomatic understatement of the *year*... she was *ancient*: her hair was entirely grey, if not white; and hung lankly about her wrinkled face. I swear she could have had no more than three teeth in her whole head... Nice person – but she was a *GRANNY!* I looked up at the sky thinking, is this your idea of a joke... of all the people! *What* have I done to deserve this...

I didn't want to hurt the old dear by taking her aside and telling her I wasn't interested. Even though I would have done it in a gentle way, the finality of hearing it could have been painful for her. So I never did raise the matter, just carried on passing the time and being friendly as before – I mean, what could she seriously expect?

A few months later, that dinner lady came to retirement age. I was provided with a photo of her and asked to do a portrait for the front of her leaving card. I was happy to oblige; in fact, it made me feel a whole lot better. I think I even put a cheeky kiss on my own dedication inside – it didn't hurt, did it – and I knew how much it would mean to her.

MINIBUS KING OF THE ROAD

It was standard practice at a certain Community College for 'A' Level Art, Graphics and Textiles students in their final year to be offered visits to the local one-year Art & Design Foundation Courses prior to deciding their Further Education options. There were three such courses in our area at that time; and each was very distinct from the others in terms of their established levels of discipline, staff-to-student ratios and individual approaches; so it was well worth the students visiting all three in order to make a sufficiently informed choice on which might suit them best.

We could easily have left the students to go on their own, a few did, but there were two reasons not to: the first being that not many of them had sufficient initiative to be that pro-active on their own behalf; and secondly because there were pertinent questions which needed to be asked of the tutors in such a way as to guide those students, via the answers given, to a decision: bombarded by the standard and variety of what they saw there, few of the partici- pants were that forthcoming; yet we, as staff, even when we already knew the answers, could very much "feed" those questions to the management in our students' presence.

The locations were all quite a way out and there happened to be a shortage of staff in the Faculty who were qualified to drive a minibus for such outings. It was common knowledge that the College happily funded anyone who wanted to take a minibus test. Even though the qualification only lasted for three years, I felt it was something worthwhile to get under my belt: the way other staff spoke about it made it seem a doddle. "Oh, they just ask you to drive a couple of times around the car park and Bob's yer uncle – you can't fail!" was how a couple of sardonic old boilers in the department put it – so I volunteered.

The test centre was in a remote location behind a set of those railway arches that garage mechanics so often favour; in a run-down, urban area of the city known as Frog Island. The fella who was assigned to assess my performance struck fear into me from the word go. He was around 6 ft 4 inches tall, with a shaved skinhead cut, and one of those deep, hard, ruthless voices that implies the owner has seen it all before and will suffer no nonsense from anyone. He wasn't unfriendly, just "rough and ready" I would say. Anyway, he got in on the passenger side, turned to me and said, "I've got a daughter who's the same age as the kids you teach; and if my arse as much as kisses this seat (strange turn of phrase), I'll fail you on the spot."

I wasn't quite sure what precisely he meant by this, but I got the general gist that he expected a smooth ride. I was already daunted by the significantly greater height at which I found myself behind the wheel of such a vehicle; but I gauged from this assessor's manner that it was wise not to show any weakness – so I kept a poker face throughout.

A couple of times around the car park? Within 30 seconds we were out in full City Centre rush-hour traffic.

"I don't like the way you're coasting up to junctions in neutral!" he remarked.

I said nothing. Kept my poker face and hoped he would think I was a confident blockhead.

As I turned off the ignition back at the test centre some 20 minutes later, he asked, "So how do you think you've done, then?"

I was almost certain he would fail me; but now that I was in character, I felt I might as well maintain the bravado to the end. "I think I've done alright," I said.

"Yep, you've passed," he answered in a matter-of-fact way – and that was that.

Many successful Foundation outings with the Sixth-Formers followed uneventfully, with myself at the wheel; although there was one occasion when, distracted by the whooping of my passengers, I misjudged a turn off the main road and one tyre struck the kerb, mounting the pavement to screams of panic from the rowdy occupants... Other than that, I think I did an ok job! Until the very last drive...

It was a cold, dark December night when, after that day's Foundation visit, having dropped the last of the students off at their requested stop – McDonalds – I returned the minibus, emblazoned with the College logo, to its home on the school campus. The hangar in which the full fleet of three identical vehicles were housed was in a rather odd position, on the edge of a hairpin bend in the driveway: rather a tricky reverse into it was required so that they were front-facing for the next day's user to drive straight out. It really was pitch-black, freezing, drizzly weather; and perhaps owing to tiredness after a full days' teaching, plus then the extra three or so hours involved in the trip, I wasn't as focused in my thinking as I should have been during the reverse. It had been a full year since the last outing and I had no memory of due procedure required to get the minibus back into the garage; I could make out nothing whatsoever in the rear-view mirror, relying totally on instinct. Surely, if I took the manoeuvre sufficiently slowly, I would feel the point at which the rear bumper made first contact with the back wall of the hangar? It never got there...

All of a sudden, in the midst of the darkness, there was the most *colossal* explosion. The noise was like nothing I had *ever* heard before – in horror I looked up to see – utter mayhem. I could make no sense out of what I saw – it seemed either the world was ending or I had gone completely insane – for all I witnessed, in the midst of this bone-shredding cacophony of noise was a myriad of colours bursting one after the other on top of each other in unimaginable brilliance as the explosions continued. It was terrifying and completely disorientating. I hunched my head down instinctively over the steering wheel, shielding it protectively with my hands – and finally, after what seemed an eternity (although it was probably only around fifteen seconds), the maelstrom of chaos, noise and light subsided. I think I must have sat there motionless, reeling in shock for a good minute before I dared get out of the driving seat. What in God's name had I done?

It wasn't until that point that it actually occurred to me that there may in fact be lights in that hangar: that's what fatigue can do to you – I should of course have switched them on before even attempting the reverse. As my fingers fumbled to find the wall-switch, the full extent of devastation was revealed. The minibus had a metal *roof-rack,* which I had reversed straight into an overhanging 6ft long white fluorescent tube – the colours had been the neon gas escaping as its glass was smashed by the collision! Finally, I could make a semblance of sense from what had happened: there was after all a rational explanation, even if the trauma had made me feel I had aged five years in those few seconds! I had no idea how much one of those lights cost, but given the size and duration of the explosion, I imagined it must run into hundreds! So it was no small relief, upon confessing all to the Premises Officer first thing the next morning, when he grinned from ear to ear and said, "Don't worry about it, mate – we're insured anyway – but they're no more than 14 or 15 squid each!"

THE TAMPON WAR

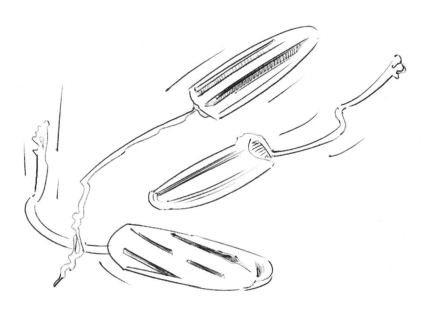

For a while, I took a number of General Cover assignments at a Community College with a tough reputation on the outskirts of the city. When it first opened, this used to be known as a "Super-school," so good was it, but then two rough inner city schools were closed and this one was obliged to absorb both populations, after which the whole place went downhill.

The days were unpredictable; most were ok; others far less so: once I came out to discover that someone had let down the tyres of my car – last thing you need at the end of a long afternoon! I sought out a foot-pump and reinflated them manually; at least the culprit hadn't gone as far as slashing them...

There then came a day when I was asked to cover one of my own ex-PGCE trainee's classes in the college's Design Faculty. The problem with any "Design" booking is that there are several different subjects hidden under that umbrella title: Art, Graphics, Textiles, Food, Electronics – and – well, it turned out that this teacher actually taught Resistant Materials (what we used to call Woodwork and Metalwork) – the practical side of which I would never have attempted to cover. Out for the day on a training course, she had left a breezy note behind, saying, "The students have all they need; I've left their equipment cupboard open, let them help themselves."

I barely had time to read this before a wiry group of Year 10's sprang through the door. It was quickly evident that there were some ongoing interpersonal issues between some of the boys in this group. Once I had registered them all, I passed on their teacher's instructions and released them to begin work. What she had neglected to forewarn me about was that, for some reason, she had left a massive box of mini-tampons inside the students' equipment cupboard! It *had* to have been an oversight on her part, because I could see the excitement the discovery generated in the boys; the tampons were a huge, illicit novelty – and within seconds, before I could do anything, the situation was out-of-hand: they were flying through the air, soaking in a sink half-filled with water – everywhere.

At once I sent a student for the On-Call member of staff. It wasn't as if the malice was particularly directed at me: I was simply an *obstacle* to those students who had an ongoing grievance with each other and were determined that their missiles should hit the enemy target! Obviously I couldn't be seen to condone what was happening, but I was on my own in the workshop, in a building some way from immediate help. I made a valiant attempt to intercede and break up the conflict, but there were two boys in particular who were playing cat-and-mouse around me trying to get to each other. Before I knew it, one of them had picked up a large rubber eraser, stuck pins into it, dunked it in some PVA glue he found at the sink, and launched it at his enemy. It struck me in the face, just below my right eye, and fell, glue-side down onto my silk shirt.

"You just got yourself an exclusion," I said.

"You're for it now," his target snickered, "Shoulda lobbed it a bit harder, mate!"

At that point, I went to the nearest classroom and brought another member of the faculty in to bawl them out. I couldn't believe the attitude of the On-Call lady who finally arrived – it was the Vice Principal; and it was as if she wanted to brush what had happened under the carpet!

"Ever heard of the self-sealing (she meant "self-*fulfilling*") prophecy, Guy?" she asked in a patronising tone.

"Are you *serious?*" I asked her, incredulously. "You would really try and palm this off on me? It's down to your own ineptitude! I sent for on-call assistance *fifteen* minutes ago."

"It's a big campus," she snapped. "We need to hurt them in their pockets. We'll get them to pay you £10 and wash your shirt – is that okay?"

"Don't get defensive," I countered. "Whether or not it was intentional, I've been *assaulted* here!"

And with that, I left.

I felt like – well, I can only make an analogy between myself and a bedraggled water-vole pursued by predators, which doggedly heads for refuge in the river bank. Its hole is barely larger than the vole itself; and it is not even as if the hole has much to offer in the way of comfort – but nonetheless, it represents "home" – and the vole aims single-mindedly for that security. With similar tunnel vision, I reached mine; and immediately called the police, who, via the college address records, went and arrested the student involved – he was excluded for a week and let off with a caution. I had one of the better agents at that time, who was extremely concerned at what had happened and went in the very next day to investigate the incident. She urged me to take time off work to recover; but I viewed it much as a parent did whose child had had a near-drowning experience at the swimming-pool: to avoid a long-term phobia developing, on the spot, he ordered his son, "Get back in the water." And in that spirit, I returned to supply work the very next morning.

Two G.P. appointments later, with £1000 compensation in my pocket, the Vice-Principal was demoted to Assistant Head: apparently her handling of the incident was the last straw in a whole catalogue of incompetence. As a result of that experience, I refused on principle to take further assignments defined only as "Design" by any school or agency: invariably, it would turn out to be Resistant Materials. You have to be specifically Health and Safety trained to teach that subject – and even if paper theory work alone is set, the students in the workshop are still in the same hazardous machine environment. One press of the wrong button – and they've potentially lost a hand.

LUNCH FOR AN ALLIGATOR

In one of my first 4+ classes, there was an irrepressible little Asian girl, who was a law unto herself. When all the other children were obediently seated, cross-legged on the carpet for Circle Time, she would suddenly crawl – lightning-fast – like a baby on all fours, over to the children on the opposite side – and would have to be returned to her original place every morning. *How* am I going to cope with this child, I wondered. She would often cut in with infant babble of her own while I was busy addressing the whole class – and after several days of this, I lost patience, turned to her sternly; and, beginning with her full name, ordered out loud, "Shut... your tiny... cake-hole!"

I looked up to see that the Headteacher had entered the room – and was standing there, shoulders shaking with laughter – luckily for me, she'd seen the funny side!

Whatever was going on, that child was insatiably curious. It was coming up for Chinese New Year; and I was making those red lucky money envelopes, *"lai see,"* with a table of children out of metallic foil. Suddenly over my shoulder, I heard, *"I want to make a Chinese envelope!"* Bless her, she was all of four years old, she barely knew what *China* was, let alone a "Chinese envelope" – but if it was happening, she was going to be part of it! Then there was another time when I was down at carpet level for some reason, cutting something out for a display; and suddenly felt something tickling the back of my head. It was her fingers – messing with my *bald* patch! At first I thought of telling her off; but knowing *that* child, if I made touching my head forbidden, it would only make it even more fascinating; so I chose to brave it out. Sure enough, after a few seconds, she lost interest, walked off – and never did it again!

A month or two later, the same little girl began wetting herself and having to be changed into spare clothes by the T.A. each day. She'd been fine at the start; there was a toilet directly down the corridor behind our room – but she'd stopped asking when she needed to go... In Gujarati, the T.A questioned her as to why she wasn't asking to go to the toilet; the lady then reported back to me that all she'd gathered was that there was something in the toilet that made the little girl scared to go in... I thought we'd better go and investigate; so at lunchtime, all three of us opened the back classroom door which led there. Admittedly, the unlit, spidery corridor was rather eerie, but this didn't appear to be the problem – it was only when we reached the toilet door that the child hesitated. So I entered the room, which was empty, apart from a sink and the toilet cubicle off to the right. I couldn't see anything out-of-the-ordinary, so I asked the child to come in with the T.A. and point to what was frightening her. Reluctantly, she did so, and pointed to the toilet cubicle. I pushed the door open. Again, nothing stood out to me, so I asked the girl gently, "What is it that's scaring you?"

With a doleful expression, she pointed to the toilet itself. It looked completely normal.

"Show me," I said – and she pointed to the seat, which was one of those old black ones.

"Is it that?" I asked; and the little girl nodded seriously. It was something about its shape or *colour,* which frightened her. That's easily solved! I thought; and managed to remove the seat from the toilet, placing it on a ledge at window height on the other side of the room. The little girl seemed brighter then; but the very next day, again she didn't ask when she needed to; and was wet again. "Is there *still* something worrying you?" I asked – and she nodded. Back to the toilet we went once more. Again, the little girl pointed to the seat on the ledge.

"It can't hurt you – it's not even on the toilet!" I said – but that wasn't good enough – the seat was still in that *room*. It wasn't until I removed it completely from the vicinity that she was comfortable enough to go to the toilet alone. As for what it was about the seat that triggered her phobia, we never did manage to discover that. Perhaps it was the blackness which scared her; or maybe it just felt freezing cold to sit on!

Our school trip later that year was to Twycross Zoo. The little girl might have been sweet, but she was also very much a handful and highly unpredictable; so I insisted her mother came along to take personal care of her child – it also helped us meet the required safety-ratio of adults to children. Making our way past frogs, toads, terrapins, snakes and lizards inside the heated Reptile House, we came to a ground-level pond, cordoned off by a clear Perspex barrier up to waist height. There on the bank crouched two motion-less alligators. Not a movement out of them – they could have been waxworks – but they weren't...

I couldn't *believe* what the mother did next. Just like that, she picked up her little girl; and in a moment uncomfortably reminiscent of Michael Jackson's heart-stopping baby-over-the-balcony blunder (and equally misjudged), she swung her up into the air, pretending to dangle the girl over the barrier. *"NO!"* I cried, the child squealed in alarm; and giggling, the mother pulled her back to safety. It was her idea of a joke. We would very rapidly have found out *just* how alive those static creatures were had she accidentally dropped the little girl inside the enclosure...

My prime objective on any trip was just to get all the children safely back to school with the requisite number of limbs intact – we very nearly *didn't* on that occasion – I hadn't bargained for one of them being offered to a pair of hungry alligators! The actions of the mother certainly shed some light on why the child behaved as she did; but you know, sometimes the naughtiest, trickiest children end up being the ones you remember with the greatest fondness!

THE GLOOMY MAN

I once inherited a Sixth Form Art class in which the students were all doing A2-size portraits of their classmates in acrylics, tempera and poster paint. There were two very laid-back lads with drawing boards, each painting the other, sitting opposite sides of the desk. I could have put *money* on them both being fairly into weed and drug-culture generally: they even spoke as if they were on a high, in that famously disinterested, chilled-out hippy tone. One of the boys in particular produced the most arresting image of the other: it was simply his head and neck against a nondescript background made up, disproportionately, of 70% blue sky and just 30% grass.

The subject's long hair was depicted in purple, with a centre parting; while the skin tones were flaming red, orange and yellow. Deep-set eyes looked up to the heavens – in which there was the weirdest-looking swirling white mass you could only ever interpret as a dope-cloud. All that was missing was a "spliff", "joint" or "Camberwell carrot" – delete as appropriate. The overall facial expression was *unutterably* gloomy – the closest resemblance it had to anyone familiar was Neil out of *The Young Ones!* Because of that, it wasn't upsetting at all to look at; it was rather comical... It wasn't thin enough to call Modigliani-inspired, but somehow, was still vaguely evocative of that artist's portraits.

These students appeared to have very scant regard for their own work; and more or less abandoned it when they left the College. The portrait had been stuck high up on one of the classroom walls; and the penetrating, gloomy eyes just seemed to follow you around the room; that fiery face and crazy-shaped white cloud grabbed my attention every day as soon as I walked in. October Half-Term was the designated cut-off date for any ex-students who wanted to pick up their old work – the rest, save a few outstanding examples, were thrown away. This painting was one of those which remained unclaimed at the end of the process; the medium used wasn't particularly well-handled, so it would hardly be retained as exemplar work; but nonetheless, there was something *so* unique about it, I just couldn't bear to see it chucked out – so home it came with me.

I had a black wood frame made for the painting, as narrow as possible, so that it wouldn't dominate over the artwork – and to this day, despite the glass being somewhat cobwebby, there on my lounge wall hangs – The Gloomy Man...

CHEF GUY

Before the local middle schools expanded to include Years 10 and 11, I covered an amazing blind teacher's Food lessons for a week. Her Golden Retriever guide dog was lovely, but was inconsolable whenever there was a thunderstorm. I particularly remember one pupil's creation, Basketball Crumble, which was drawn in response to a brief instructing them to create their own imaginary dish – it was nothing if not that – with the stitched leather balls shown erupting out of the top layer.

I was quite nervous at first about the "makes" in front of the pupils, as cooking is far from my own field of expertise; but decided I would try and carry it off with a veneer of bluster, charisma and false confidence. I got hold of one of those classic long chef's hats and a big white apron; and wore them for the whole week, flinging the classroom door open with gusto to disarm and welcome each class. It seemed to work. I figured however little I knew, it was probably more than most of them; many had never even used a broom before and had to be taught how to sweep up after themselves! The pupils just wanted someone with enthusiasm, who made the processes seem exciting and easy. The fact I had learned each method barely five minutes before they came through the door was entirely unknown to them. I made them say, "Yes, Chef," rather than "Sir" – it amused me, as I knew I was actually such a talentless cook.

Fruit salads were great fun, but the most memorable lesson of all was pizza-making. The pupils were able to buy pre-filled polystyrene cupfuls of topping for 30p; but one became intensely competitive about having the largest pizza. He paid £3 and poured 10 cupfuls of cheese onto his base; turning it into a bizarre alien hemisphere. It seemed to alter state entirely, metamorphosing into a bubbling, sentient mass of molten plasma. I wouldn't have liked to be the one cleaning his oven out.

SELF-DEPRECATING HUMOUR

The first year of the old 'A' Level Art & Design: Graphics course was all about students experimenting as far as possible in their set projects with different media and techniques; both to build their expertise and add more to their creative repertoire. In their sketch-books and worksheets, they were expected to explain in writing what they were doing at every stage. One of them, a very low-ability student, made me roar with involuntary laughter while I was marking his work... I turned a page to find this muddy, shapeless mess, at the side of which were the biro-scrawled, self-effacing words, "Here, I tried covering tissue paper with different-coloured inks. I thought it would make it look better – but I was wrong."

The student knew deep down that he wasn't all that great on the Art and Design side and probably shouldn't have taken the subject.

Giving him his feedback, I told him, "While it may be an 'E' on the project itself, I'd definitely give you a grade 'A' for your sense of humour!" – which at least elicited an accepting smile.

TONGUEMAN

I was telephoned rather late on a Monday morning to come and fill in for a middle school Graphics teacher who had been signed off sick for two weeks. The resident Head of Department, a great fella I had once mentored as a P.G.C.E student, had come up with the idea of a 'Design Your Own Superhero' project, which actually played right into my hands; as I had recently been burned by an identical-ly-themed prank of mine which had got out of hand in the next-door Senior school! In that college, it had been announced in Staff Briefing that the Pastoral Heads had received very few entries and a poor response from the students to a challenge in which they were asked to create an 'Anti-Bullying' superhero. To encourage competition, in a few spare minutes, I decided to create a 'spoof' entry, based on a long-running, copyrighted 'alter-ego' of mine – 'Tongueman.'

The titular hero did not in fact have either a cloak, a logo on his chest or any other accessories typical of the classic superhero: the strength of his blandness being that he could blend with a crowd and suddenly emerge from them to deal with any bullying incident at the very moment it reared its ugly head. The only thing which made him extraordinary was his *enormously* long tongue, also known as the 'Pink Pacifier;' which of course wouldn't be seen until he opened his mouth. It would then shoot out a ray of Instant Karma; and the bullies would be restrained in a pool of ultra-adhesive Subduing Saliva; and made to admit the errors of their ways before they were released. Bullying incidents could be written down in detail and posted through one of Tongueman's 'Let's Lick it!' boxes positioned around the building. These would be regularly emptied by his discreet undercover team of student assistants known as 'The Taste Buds,' who would inform their superior of the details in due haste.

On a single sheet of A4, I submitted this idea – anonymously – with a drawing to Student Support; but a few days later, much to my shock, it was announced in front of the entire college staff that, although they had no idea whose entry it was, the superhero chosen as a mascot to head the Anti-Bullying campaign was... Tongueman – and could tutors please find out from their students who the artist was. He'd only gone and *won!* Several of my colleagues already knew that the character was one of my own more outlandish creations; and one or two of the women didn't like him, claiming the tongue looked "a bit sexual" – they were muttering under their breath and looking disapprovingly in my direction – so I had to go and guiltily 'fess up to Student Support, who took the news very graciously!

Obviously, the idea was for a student – not a teacher – to win the competition; and I think the whole thing was shelved after that... But when I drew and annotated him on the whiteboard, the middle school pupils doing the superhero project took to Tongueman immediately: he motivated them to produce some highly-inventive and varied superheroes of their own; the most unusual of which was "The Munter" – a large, T-shirted pupil so hideously ugly that he would stop bullies in their tracks and make their jaws drop open with his hideousness – giving the victim time to escape and the bullies a chance to reflect on their actions.

INCLUSION

What I write here is bound to be divisive, and will probably be seen by many as "un-PC" – that's fine – people are welcome to disagree with me; it's just my own personal view, borne of 25 years' direct experience. Let me be clear: I have nothing against children with physical disabilities of any kind – I've worked on a specialist summer camp with them; I also have a lot of empathy with those on the autistic spectrum. But severe anti-social *behavioural* issues I find more of a struggle to sympathise with.

When I first began my teaching career, the vast majority of such children were taught in special schools. Due to cuts in government funding, plus the current policy of inclusion, the thinking became, "no – let's, let's *integrate* them – they've got a right for their school experience to be as normalised as possible" – so most are now included in mainstream school. It's almost as if one bad apple – or more – is systematically rationed out to spoil just about every class. It's tragic...

They disrupt lessons, take a massively disproportionate share of the teacher's attention; and because staff would be firing on all cylinders if they reacted to every misdemeanour, often only the most major get addressed. This leads to inequality, causing other pupils in the class to question why *they* themselves should get disciplined, when the child in question gets away with the same, or similar, offence. I've been required to endure students coming into my classes and disturbing them from day one, screaming apropos of nothing at 10-second intervals (making whole-class teaching almost impossible) and putting everyone on edge. I've had them climb onto table-tops, destroy classroom equipment or artwork on display, grab women teachers in the face, slander me with gay accusations; and accomplish little or nothing in lesson time.

Most important of all, in 99% of cases, they *don't* end up feeling "normal" as intended. The vast majority of these "challenging" individuals are simply unable to keep up with the pace of the class; and often, special, differentiated work has to be pre-prepared for them, adding to the teacher's already busy workload. The pupil just ends up feeling even more different – not normal at all: it's flawed thinking!

Possibly the toughest encounter I had with students of this kind was when a pastoral crisis arose at a former place of work. They had agreed to take on eight or nine very extreme students referred to as the "Nurture Group." These were pupils who were off-timetable doing more vocational activities with their own dedicated behaviour support teacher; who happened to be the brother of a current, golden footballing hero both in the media and on television – an absolute household name. The teacher, a highly popular giant of a man, had spent a year building up a good rapport with the Nurture Group, they really looked up to him and were beginning to respond – and then very abruptly, at the end of the academic year, an invitation to go on tour with his celebrity brother came up, which he felt he could not refuse. And, quite controversially, he had resigned suddenly, without notice – at least no term-time notice.

At the start of the new year, the Nurture Group had found him to be gone, with a quiet-natured, elderly man in his place to whom they did not respond well at all. They were genuinely upset, felt abandoned and betrayed, and in response, had totally given up – and played up. The new teacher had, by his own admission, lost his rag completely with them, told the Principal he felt way out of his depth – and stepped down. At this point, I was offered the job by way of a temporary fix, but much of the crucial key detail was kept from me. It truly was a poisoned chalice.

You did not feel safe with those students. They burst suddenly into the room, sending computer equipment flying as they tussled with each other; I was just an irrelevance to them. The most menacing among them was actually the smallest: he was out on bail awaiting a court case for GBH, having attacked someone on the street and broken their jaw; he couldn't be reasoned with and, with a slow build-up, would scream "r-rr-AAAGGH!" every few seconds. Perhaps there was an element of Tourette's there, but the assault on one's nerves was devastating, leaving both myself and the others constantly on edge.

Another of the group had to be sent home in a taxi every day as an enemy was suspected to have taken a knife from home and was waiting daily for the opportunity to kill him outside the school gates. I didn't give up on them entirely, but their Form Tutor had to pitch in and we had a rough and ready ex-con Teaching Assistant intro-duced, who was respected for his gym experience. That was the only thing that really held any kudos for the Nurture Group: macho, ego-building sessions where I would find myself wearing a padded focus mitt, the recipient of frenzied punches; any one of which, had it gone astray accidentally or deliberately, could have resulted in serious injury... They didn't seem to get much out of any activity – it really was a case of containment more than anything. The only memorable task they achieved was washing a staff-member's car – and only that until a policeman on the beat from the school unit appeared, resulting in them walking off the job in disgust, shouting, "The Feds! The Feds!"

It's only really time and familiarity which result in any rapport being built with pupils like this. It might be "just the way things are" right now; and forgive me if it seems a ruthless, outdated or intol-erant viewpoint, but my opinion has always been this: one has to weigh up the rights of any disturbed individual to their education against those of many, many others to an *undisturbed* one – and my vote I'm afraid, will always go with the majority. There should be no place in mainstream school for severely disruptive or challenging students – no matter what their underlying conditions.

PARENTING

In the Nursery of an Infant school I visited regularly, I used to work with the most wonderful, inspiring and petite African-Caribbean Christian lady. She was a talented singer and acoustic guitar-player; and had made up little songs for everything she asked the children to do.

"Nel-son, Nel-son, go and get your coat", "Come to the carpet", etc. The Foundation 1 children adored her and couldn't wait to hear their names being sung out: off they would toddle and obediently perform whatever was asked. I borrowed that idea and used it, along with a piano keyboard, in many other Early Years classes.

So at home was that lady in the Nursery environment, she would take off her shoes and go barefoot at carpet-level with the children. She was there, day-in, day-out for almost 20 years... I admired both her and her commitment tremendously; and beyond the school gates, she became a valued friend. Later, I happened to teach both her daughter and son Art at secondary school. He was getting into bad company at one point; and I was able to be his mum's eyes and ears, alerting her to his deteriorating behaviour early on, which she nipped very firmly in the bud. Equally, she and another co-worker were really there for me later on in a personal crisis; for which I remain eternally grateful.

One day, while we were both out on break-duty in the playground, we happened to touch on the subject of the thousands of children I must have taught.

"Didn't you ever want children of your own?" she asked me.

"I think my views on that change every now and then..." I murmured, reflecting on the question. "Parenting's an altogether different relationship from Teaching; although there's a similar element of care involved, it's not the same – I'm always very happy to hand those children back at the end of the day. I think the enormity of responsibility bringing up a child is just too scary for me – I can barely regulate my own life, let alone anyone else's! And I suppose, because mine has always been full of children, via work, I've never really felt a "gap" there; that I've missed out by not having kids of my own..."

Without at all intending to, I must have sounded a little wistful at that moment; for then she said, "You know, though, in your own way, Guy – you actually *are* a parent... really, you are." It was not strictly true, but that's the way she put it; it was an incredibly sweet thing to say, which stayed in my mind a long time – I was very touched.

The community college I went to next had a plaque in the Staffroom which they had put up for Black History Month, asking visitors to write on it those people they felt had been most influential. Some famous names had been written, such as Malcolm X, Stevie Wonder and Barack Obama – all very worthy – but before I left, having given thought to it for several weeks, I took up the pen which hung there on a string and, in a quiet moment when no-one else was in the room, wrote that lady's name up, along with the reasons why. In that category, it was, after all, *she* who had had the greatest impact on me.

ACTIVISM

Aside from the recently-established Agency Workers Regulations (AWR) which aim to guarantee parity pay to Teachers Pay Scale if you work in the same school 12 weeks or more (of *zero* benefit if you are a day-to-day specialist and move around as I did – you then have little chance of ever reaching that 12 weeks); there's virtually no regulation of the conditions supply teachers work under. How you get paid will depend entirely on the agency you work for. Most supplies would far rather be paid by schools and local authorities directly; and greatly object to agencies charging extortionate fees on top of what they get paid. It's a total rip-off.

The teachers do a full day's work, but the agent makes barely one phone call, which hardly justifies their fee. Many school staff are unaware of this mark-up, so the supply teacher encounters both office and teaching staff antagonism for being so expensive – when in fact they earn a *fraction* of the total cost charged to schools and, in order to get assignments, are compelled to accept pay rates way lower than their actual entitlement.

Both the status and pay of supply teachers needs to be raised exponentially: after all, how long could the education system survive *without* us? Over the years, in response to continuous urging from others in the same plight, I became increasingly vocal via demonstrations about conditions in supply teaching; it was of course my democratic right; but even so, I only ever attended one public demonstration, in 2017. So paranoid was I about being identified and losing the little work that I had, that I disguised myself in a waterproof anorak with a cap underneath to alter the shape of my head; along with dark sunglasses and a Victorian music-hall-style handlebar moustache. My best friend gasped in disbelief when he saw the photos. It certainly wasn't my intention, but, "You look more like an ISIS *terrorist* than a demonstrator!" he remarked.

We stood at the centre of town with placards, stickers for the general public and a petition for them to sign; then walked to several of the biggest agencies to demonstrate outside. The agency staff barricaded themselves indoors and refused to come out to talk to us; so the head union rep went in to confront them instead.

The greatest irony is that, at a time when I was effectively unemployed (although not claiming benefits), I probably had the greatest degree of public exposure in my life: in the same 10-day period, I was quoted in The Guardian newspaper ("Why supply teachers need a better deal") *and* was recruited directly through the N.U.T to be interviewed on BBC Radio 4's *Money Box* programme about the pressure put on supply teachers to join offshore umbrella payroll schemes.

I am far from an activist by nature, but this was a situation of the agencies' own making: treat any workforce poorly and they will rise up – that is exactly what happened: *they* created the monster.

The risk in involving yourself in any such action though, is that it is always very much your own head over the parapet: while it was never stated outright, I have little doubt that in certain agencies I was categorised as a 'troublemaker' from then on; resulting in a total end to my day-to-day offers of work. It all comes down to how far you are prepared to make a stand for any cause you believe in – regardless of the possible consequences to yourself.

CUPID'S ARROW AND THE ANTI-MALE ENVIRONMENT

Wherever people work together, it is inevitable that feelings of attraction can develop, regardless of how professional one endeavours to be. At a local infant school in which I was booked for most of the year, I found myself in a *desperate* situation: I had fallen in love with a young, newly-qualified staff-member who was on a long-term temporary contract. It would have been unethical even had it been reciprocated – but she was not available... In all my time as a teacher, such a thing had never occurred; it was a truly unexpected situation which was *shattering* for me. No-one can anticipate such powerful emotions; I never planned it – the girl barely made an impression on me the first day I met her, but six months later, turned my whole world upside-down.

I had left temporarily to do a short maternity cover; and just before the start of the new academic year, went in to see my agent, who asked me if I remembered the girl. I hadn't a clue who she was talking about. "Well, you've certainly got an admirer there, Mr Guy," was all she said. How *could* that teacher have slipped under my radar... Upon seeing her again for the first time, I felt as if I had been hit head-on by a train... Not only was she *tiny*; and quite bewitchingly beautiful, she was wise and self-possessed beyond her years, earnestly committed to her work and with an utterly compelling poignant side that I felt compelled to understand and support. People are not objects – I know that – but nonetheless she was – *the* – single, most captivating thing I ever saw in my life. My heart would leap; literally miss a beat whenever I saw her: she was like a jewel at the centre of the chaperoning entourage that always seemed to flank her protectively when she walked up the corridor modelling the latest Cheryl Cole fashions; hair shining like a shampoo ad and her proud, pointy little chin upright – it was as if she had come from another planet. Every lunchtime she seemed to vanish into thin air (though I suspect she may just have skipped off the premises for a quick smoke!) – and never once did I see her eat. She broke up with her boyfriend later on in the year and confided in me a lot; there wasn't the *slightest* physical contact from me, she might have squeezed my arm a couple of times, but that was it... nonetheless, it was the most powerful attraction I simply could not fight.

I know how easy it is to delude oneself that something is there when it is not; but certainly our communication was a two-way thing – close to 400 texts between us, plenty with kisses from her, sent at the very time she used to speak to her ex before falling asleep; and several hour-long phone calls from her to me. I would make her silly things; she would sneak out of her class to call me when I wasn't in the school, or send little children up to my room with private messages when I was. Don't get me wrong, it was far from all bad; when things were going well between us, I was in absolute ecstasy: she must have rang and texted me on eight or nine separate occasions one birthday from morning to night; I was so blissfully happy at those times... By my own admission I was very, very shy, but her sweet response was simply "I'll do the talking..." There was an undeniable tenderness; a mutual looking-out for each other both during the school day and alone in her classroom afterwards; in whatever ways I could alleviate her workload, I would; hearing her readers, creating artwork displays she couldn't manage herself; and giving her advice and support with her interview technique.

She was the centre of attention for the school's only male teacher: me; and at one point, completely mistook my coming to speak privately with her as a marriage-proposal – from which I back-pedalled frantically! – however, in hindsight, I realise she was probably the first candidate worthy of genuine consideration.

It felt at the time like the *deepest* of connections; like a physical pull; we were drawn to each other by something way bigger than both of us; which neither of us had the words to fully articulate. And I was desperate – I felt I had the narrowest of windows in which to win her heart before she was snapped up by someone else – the time felt as if it was slipping hopelessly away like sand through my fingers...

Unquestionably, it was 100% my fault for not taking avoiding action and asking my agent to find me work elsewhere; but I just couldn't face the prospect of never seeing that girl again – besides, it was my only regular school and I needed the work. With no end in sight, the situation was devastating to me; it was taking all my strength and willpower just to get through each day. The slightest glimpse of her, even from a distance, was, quite literally, wounding to me – it was *Shakespearean* in its intensity – I have never known such raging want for another human being; she drove me almost out of my mind.

I think that only happens to you once, maybe twice in your life... Perhaps it was indeed a "mid-life crisis" – I was extremely shaken up, frightened and bewildered by what I was experiencing. I thought I was going crazy and felt there was nobody I could turn to or confide in at the school. My sparkle was gone; and many were the times I simply broke down in private, seeking refuge in a stockroom, cloakroom or walk-in cupboard – anywhere I would not be seen crying. I was the only man in that all-female environment; and totally unable to control what I was feeling. It is not always easy for us fellows to talk about such things; nor was it mere fleeting infatuation. At one point I had lost over a stone in weight. I could hardly function at the weekends, barely getting off the sofa for thinking of her; and when she texted me, I would pray for the right words – any words – that might sway her and win her heart... I was unable even to face staff nights out; being at the same table as this individual, yet unable to communicate or even look her way, was too painful. For the first time, I felt a major conflict of interest between my professional and personal life. I did my best not to let it affect my teaching; but it remained a real dilemma for which I could not find a solution – with the exception perhaps of time and distance.

There is far more openness nowadays to talk about feelings; but back then, I really did not consider professional help an option; nor was I prepared to face the stigma which still existed with regard to seeking it. I did, luckily, have friends beyond work to confide in; and I was still close to my ex-girlfriend, who was really supportive. The teacher herself tried as hard as she could to be as accommodating as possible under very difficult circumstances; but realistically, we just couldn't be friends. She kept me hanging on only until she had achieved certain career and relationship goals; then immediately began avoiding all contact in school. Understandably I suppose, soon after that, all external contact between the girl and myself also came to a rather acrimonious end.

I never breathed a word to anyone there about the situation – the girl concerned valued discretion in our contact above everything and had sworn me to secrecy – but she herself may not have adhered to that same confidentiality. I had long suspected that certain humourless, embittered souls among the staff would be glad to obtain the slightest leverage to see the back of me; somehow someone found out about the situation, influenced others; and they all closed ranks over a private, personal issue; something that was really none of their concern and would be equally beyond their control had they found themselves in a similar scenario. All you can do in any such circumstance is hope people can balance the good they know about you against whatever malicious gossip is spread behind your back.

On the last day I worked there, the atmosphere was perceptibly frosty: with the exception of a tiny handful, I was made to feel acutely unwelcome. Even lovely staff I usually got on well with averted their eyes, turned their backs – even though I could see they were torn doing it – effectively, they sent me to Coventry. I even saw one teacher nudge a cook, then point to me in the lunch-queue – my ears were burning; rumour-spreading of "harassment" was rife. One particular individual had, for years, been inexplicably off with me, oblivious to anything I contributed, especially in children's presence; and, even on occasions, openly rude and abrupt; all of which I had tried to overlook. In my very last encounter with her on a corridor, she smiled with clear menace; and having never returned a greeting before, said, in a sarcastic, *Weakest Link* tone, "Goodbye!" The inference was clear: it really *is* goodbye: we've *got* something on you now...

One thing is for certain: gender-discrimination was alive and thriving in that school: I know for a fact I was not the only male employee who had encountered similar cold-shoulder treatment. There was an ongoing campaign aimed at the defamation of my character; a concerted attempt to besmirch my good name. Even at the end of assembly, precisely as I would turn my back to lead a class out, there would be a loud, simulated gasp of horror – not from a child, but from an anonymous member of *staff* – each time implying some unspeakable act on my part, like inappropriate physical contact. It was a *huge* mistake that not once did I turn and challenge them publicly: "*Who* was that?" – insisting on knowing why – but always, I was too intimidated to do so. I had no idea who it was; and it would have made a major scene in front of the children in my care. Each 'gasp' was apropos of *nothing* – nor were there ever grounds for such expressions of horror at a thing I did in my teaching career: in fact I would often recount to others how sad were the lengths I felt compelled to go to in order to ensure absolutely zero ambiguity contact-wise, *not* returning hugs in the playground for instance, when infants who knew me would run up and fling their arms around me in greeting; but instead feeling I had to stand with arms outstretched and rigid – and to this day, I still carry a spotless Enhanced Disclosure certificate (DBS). But that staff gasp happened on no less than *three* separate occasions; the aim, I am sure, being "throw a little mud, some'll stick", "no smoke without fire", etc.

Sounds like paranoia, but I prefer the term heightened awareness. Antagonism to male staff working in the Infant/Primary sector can be quite insidious and covert, yet *absolutely* real: I cannot stress enough the need for senior management in those particular schools to ensure all staff recognise the need to welcome and appreciate those rare men who dare venture in. An entrenched perception still exists that we lack the necessary caring or nurturing skills for that setting. Small wonder there are so few of us who remain in it for any length of time! Perhaps I was just one more statistic, subtly frozen out, partly driven, by a close-knit core of anti-male staff on the lookout for any ammunition whatsoever to twist to their own ends. It was not the first time I had encountered such an undercurrent: the whole phenomenon needs investigating in real depth; research is essential, because there is no question it exists.

If experience of such intimidation turns out to be a nationwide trend for men in Infant/Primary schools; and if the resulting absence of sufficient male role-models can even in part be attributed to an unwelcoming culture, it has *enormously* damaging implications for teacher-retention; not to mention acceptance of the very education process by some pupils in those crucial early years. Perhaps that whole motivational "switch-off" leading to girls overtaking boys academically is triggered at a far earlier age than recognised. The very learning-resistance thought to stem from insufficient endorsement by male role-models could well be due to an endemic, hostile climate putting off so many potentially excellent male recruits!

The girl involved could never have imagined the extremes I contemplated once she ended contact. I had a routine hernia operation the following year, with a general anaesthetic from which I hoped I would never wake up: I just couldn't see myself ever being happy again. She alone could have made a stand against the defamatory things said against me; but she never did. I was just a stepping-stone towards her getting where she wanted to be: back with her ex; safe in a permanent job. At its simplest, I was naive – and I was used.

She did serve a purpose in my life, though, because with her, I hit rock bottom: no-one will *ever* hurt me to that degree again – so the only way is up! I've been in new relationships since; but from that day to this, without fail, out comes her name from my mouth as I fall asleep: at some unconscious level she remains hard-wired into my brain.

Both privately and financially, it was a tough year. The ending of my most regular source of day-to-day work ultimately led to the loss of my home, which had to be put on the market; all I could afford to downgrade to was a one-bedroom bungalow. I had visited that school for seven years, happy ones, for the most part; and the Head herself was a wonderful, balanced Sikh lady. Without naming names, I wrote to her about everything, but I never got a reply. The wider concerns ought really to have been raised collectively with the whole staff; but any allegation brought to her may have changed her opinion of me for the worse; and she would have felt duty-bound to listen to her regular employees. All I could do was hope that her usual calm and reasoned judgment had not been swayed by some twisting or stretching of the truth by those with their own agenda.

However strongly staff may have felt that their side-taking was justified, I gave my all to that school; and at the end of the day, I was only human; I did my best to stay professional under circumstances of tremendous emotional distress. I never let it affect my dealings with the children; but the whole atmosphere felt tainted after that; even if another assignment had come in, the school could only ever have been a pale shadow of the enjoyable place it once was – so I never went back: a most unfortunate turn of events; and a salutary lesson for *everyone* on the need for alertness regarding professional distance.

THE PLAYSCHEME

For five consecutive years, before funding was withdrawn and it ceased to exist, I led the 5-7 year-olds' Summer Playscheme for the University of Leicester. It was great fun; and many of the same children and assistants returned time and time again – I don't think we had a single falling-out or scrap to deal with in the entire five years. There were no real lessons to speak of; all I had to do was create a range of craft activities, such as mask-making, make stencils of pop-stars who were currently all the rage and draw some exciting photocopiable pictures for the children to colour. All the activities were carried out in a single, designated room with a wall-mounted television in the corner tuned to MTV; so it was always lively and buzzing with noise. But that was only a tiny facet of the playscheme; a full schedule of day-trips out was preplanned.

My main duty was just to lead these expeditions and oversee the safe return of all the children. Sometimes the coaches would simply take them, along with a packed lunch, to a local green space in which to expend energy on the park rides; there might be supervised swimming at a nearby pool; or a Drama session with University undergraduates. I clearly recall one such session with an inexperienced student in charge, who became increasingly agitated when her instruction to "Freeze!" was repeatedly ignored by the excited infants!

Other days though were far more ambitious and we would end up having a blast at either Drayton Manor or Alton Towers. The only real failure to speak of was a day-trip to Dudley Zoo: the coach got caught up in a horrendous traffic-jam on the M5; there were no toilet facilities on board and we were stuck on the road for three hours. By the time we finally arrived, the children only had 40 minutes both to eat their lunch *and* see the animals – they then had to endure another three-hour journey back! Not one of them complained – but the fact no-one had an accident on board the whole day was a near-miracle...

My most potent memory of all regarding the playschemes, though, was the attendance, one year, of a tiny Chinese boy, who was happy and well-adjusted right through the experience – until the day came when we were scheduled to visit the Tales of Robin Hood attraction in Nottingham. If I remember rightly, this took the form of some kind of automated chair-lift of log-effect buggies which each group sat in. They would then rattle through a succession of elaborate tableaux featuring mannequins in medieval costume; each depicting more of the famous outlaw's antics with his Merry Men in Sherwood Forest. What no-one had told us, however, was that this child was absolutely *terrified* of the dark: within seconds of the ride beginning outside in broad daylight, it plunged into blackness – and he began *screaming* at the top of his voice.

I did my best to calm the boy down and to distract him by pointing out all the exciting, illuminated features we were passing – but to no avail. He just would not stop crying; and I knew I had to get him out of there before he worked himself into hysteria – or worse. Clearly the attraction was not set up for any such emergency exit mid-ride:

it proved no easy task to leave our particular buggy, which had quite high sides; and the boy had to be passed down to me. We then had to find our way out through the labyrinth without being run over by any other passing carriages! Obviously there was no way I could leave a tiny infant unattended with strangers, particularly in his state; so I just had to stand outside with him until the rest of the participants rejoined us.

Later that same week, the Grand Finale on the last day was a trip to the cinema to see the latest children's blockbuster: *George of the Jungle* or something. All the children were incredibly excited and hyped-up about the trip, but after what had happened, I should have anticipated the darkness inherent in any visit to the movies... The moment the lights went down, the Chinese boy began screaming inconsolably again – once more I had to take him outside and wait with him the full 80 minutes until the film finished – I think I had well and truly had my fill of the Playscheme after that...

WORKPLACE BULLY

I thought you might be interested to hear how I tackled this particular situation; as it's something that could potentially happen to anyone at some point in their working life. I'm not saying my choice of strategy here was necessarily the *right* one; people may well disagree with me and argue that I should have taken a stronger stance or a different approach – it's something individual that anyone finding themselves in a similar situation would have to make their own mind up about. But it's certainly a thought-provoking anecdote, whichever side of the fence you are on.

Out of the blue, some eight years after moving on from my permanent Graphics position, I was head-hunted back by my old place of work. They were in a predicament, having had to sack a new maternity-cover employee on the spot after finding she had forged her qualifications in league with her partner, who worked in an agency. Not only was she fired, he was also then given the sack by his place of work. The whole situation had turned nasty and now all the forger's classes were without a teacher. I was only too happy to cover the full six-months; as not only was supply work becoming increasingly sporadic, I myself was starting to flag after years of non-stop primary assignments – my brain just needed a higher level of stimulation!

Things had moved on considerably since my day, but incredibly, some of the worksheets I had designed back then were still in regular use. Graphics was now run by a husband-and-wife team; it was she who was off on maternity leave. Several of the most senior Design Faculty staff were still there; truly wonderful, dedicated people, every one of them; and even just at human level, such lovely, warm, sincere folk. They were rather relieved to have me back; and I was more-or-less fêted like royalty when I arrived; so was able to negotiate exemption from certain aspects of the job I found onerous, such as meetings. I think the continuing presence of the old guard actually helped keep the new fella in charge of Graphics in check; he could see I was someone valued by those above him; and we got on well enough; even doing occasional team-teaching – so by and large, the six months went by relatively uneventfully.

Three years on, however, when I was sought out yet again to cover a second maternity leave for the same woman, things felt very, *very* different... By this time, both the Head of Faculty and most of the other staff I had known had either retired or moved on; and there was an altogether changed 'vibe' to the atmosphere: everyone there was still just as dedicated as before; and both old and new faces worked at least as hard; but somehow, the department didn't seem to *cohere* quite as well as before; and it was a markedly less happy place to be – the smiling and joking had all-but gone.

The most marked difference of all, though, was in the Head of Graphics himself. Although several years younger than me, he had become a very brooding figure who could lose his temper with students and bristle, visibly, if you asked him for assistance with even the most trivial thing. His wife had just given birth to their second child; and while I am sure those 3 a.m. feeds must have been a contributory factor, it still didn't excuse his surly manner. Very gradually, over a period of the first two months of my cover, he became more and more difficult to approach or deal with; the status of his now being Head of Department seemed to have gone to his head; and, not physically, you understand, but in a more insidious, verbal way, he began to try and push me around; becoming very dictatorial about the way things were done.

It all reached a head one Friday afternoon after lessons had finished; when he suddenly dumped several hours' worth of data (something he particularly knew I hated!) on my desk for me to input into the system; along with a warning that, from now on, he was going to put a much heavier workload and weight of responsibility on my shoulders. The worst thing was that I have a tendency *not* to be present to how I should be reacting in the moment itself (things tend to hit me later), so I actually sat and *took* what was going on without saying a word! Home he went, and I sat there until 6.30 p.m. inputting that data. But it wasn't so much the task which bothered me as much as his general manner. I could see that, unless I asserted myself and stood up to the man – fast – to show him I was no pushover, things could only continue to worsen. No way was I going to let myself become the victim of bullying in any workplace – let alone *my* old stamping-ground!

The problem was on my mind the entire weekend. It wasn't a happy one; but I spoke to no-one about the situation – just turned it over and over methodically in my head – until finally, I narrowed my options down to three:

Option 1: I could do nothing.

Option 2: I could raise a formal complaint.

Option 3: I could have a private 1:1 chat with the chap about the situation.

Looking at the pros and cons of each strategy, if I chose Option 1 – doing nothing – then for sure, the fella would see me as soft. He would carry out his threat, increase my workload exponentially and lose all respect for me – which may lead to even worse repercussions, perhaps developing into full-on public bullying.

If I chose Option 2 – raising a formal complaint – several things would happen. First, whether or not there was a meeting, hearing or tribunal of any kind, there would inevitably be a delay in addressing the complaint – a date or time set, etc. The news would be bound to result in significant resentment on his part – he would hate me. Other colleagues would be bound to take sides – either overtly or covertly – and we would still have every full, busy day of work with the students to get through – with an awful atmosphere adding to the pressure. Not only that: with him in a position of seniority, there was no guarantee my grievance would even be upheld. He would have time to make up justifications prior to the hearing; and if it didn't go my way, I could come out of the situation even worse off.

And if I chose Option 3 – having a private chat with him on a 1:1 basis – well, that was the scariest of all, confronting him directly, *but* – if the tables were turned and it was me being challenged for my behaviour, I think that is the approach I would most respect – that the person with the grievance *hadn't* gone over my head, "grassed" (as it might be viewed) and stirred up a load of trouble for me; but had instead kept the matter between ourselves and sought a resolution man-to-man. That was the option I was most inclined to take; but if I went down that route, I would have to be very, very clear and concise about what I actually said – effectively building a sufficient case that couldn't be argued with; and taking him off-guard at a time he might least expect. That was what I decided to do...

I felt it was crucial that I should already be established at my desk when he walked through the door – so I got up especially early that morning and made sure I was. In flounced the fella through the door, a quarter of an hour later; just a little too 'matey' and friendly I felt to be genuine; perhaps he knew he had overstepped the mark the Friday before; hence there was an element of over-compensation going on.

"How you doing, Guy?" he asked brightly. "Good weekend?"

As a statement rather than a question, the first thing I said was, "Can I have a word in private."

I could see he was taken aback a second or two; almost certainly he had an inkling why I may have asked; but he made a valiant attempt to appear unfazed, saying in a lightweight tone, "Course you can, mate! Just let me grab a coffee and we'll go through..."

I chose one of the studios with a closed door, rather than the open-plan area; and we took stools and sat down. There was no way to beat around the bush: I had to be direct.

"To cut a long story short," I began, "I wasn't happy with the way you spoke to me last Friday."

"I know, I know," he said, gulping visibly. "I almost rang you over the weekend, actually."

"I felt I had three options here," I continued (and I cited them exactly as above). "It seemed far better to try and keep things between the pair of us and sort it out man-to-man without anyone else getting involved. You might think as a supply, that I've got a lot less on my plate than the rest of you; but I feel the pressure just as much as the next man – I might not show it – but I do. And I don't know if you realise, but it was actually me that started off the 'A' Level Graphics course at this college right at the beginning – *years* before you or your wife even set foot in the building... You probably wouldn't even have your jobs if it wasn't for me; and last thing I'm going to do is sit back and let you think you can pile a whole 'notha layer of pressure on my shoulders...

"No-one's going to push me around – all I'm asking for is a little bit of professional respect and mutual goodwill. I don't expect my head bitten off, for instance if I make a routine request for information, such as how to work a Faculty camera where there are no instructions. The only thing – the *only* thing – that actually stopped me going over your head and making a formal complaint is my awareness that you are almost certainly, *massively* sleep-deprived – and for that, I've made allowances."

I couldn't believe the response this elicited. He was a big fella, this bloke, but in that moment, he just looked totally undone; and instantly acknowledged what I was saying.

"No – you're 100% right, Guy," he said, quietly. "I was out of order – and... I apologise."

"That's *all* I wanted to hear," I said, standing up to leave. "I shan't mention it again."

It cleared the air – and was very, very necessary. I wasn't hostile about it; just assertive – and he never gave me any trouble – or data! – again. I actually spotted the poor fella shooting a quick, surreptitious glance at me over the rim of his tea-cup that break time. Normally someone ultra-confident, who would physically spread himself out and was almost cocky even in his body language, the look in his rolling eyes at that moment was reminiscent of a spooked horse: I am not saying it's an emotion I sought to elicit particularly, but what I saw in those eyes in that briefest nano-second – was *fear*. In that single meeting, the balance of power had shifted – and I knew I had made the right decision.

THE ALTERNATIVE BIRTHDAY CAKE

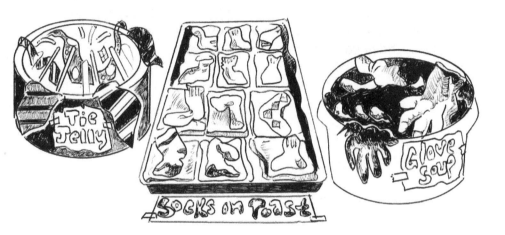

It was a welcome tradition in the Design Staffroom for people to bring in a cake on their birthday to share with the other staff at break time. We were seldom short of it in our Faculty and it never failed to raise everyone's spirits; helping us all to get through the rest of the morning. There were people from other departments all over the college who appeared to have almost a radar for every such occasion; and who would descend, uninvited, for a hefty slice, right on cue – much to the disgruntled, under-breath mutterings of certain, less charitable members of staff who didn't appreciate the regularity of the impostors!

I brought in a cake too for the first three years, but then, being the prankster I am, decided it would be amusing to shake everyone up – not in a *nasty* way, you understand – just subvert the birthday cake tradition enough to rattle the applecart of conventionality and watch people's reactions. So the night before, I conjured up three surreal dishes to bring in the next morning: *socks on toast* (all

149

meticulously buttered), *tie jelly* (with a slimy, motley collection over-hanging the rim of the bowl); and, most repulsive of all, *glove soup* (heavy outdoor workman's gauntlets, semi-embedded in a cold, grey, mushroom gloop).

The aim was to be as dead-pan as possible when offering to ladle out these dishes to the staff – however, in most cases, my tendency to burst out laughing ended up betraying me. No-one recoiled in horror or went as far as playing along and accepting a plateful; but they did all generously see the funny side, declining graciously with a good-natured giggle or smile. I had, of course, brought the real deal in as well (hidden from sight under the counter) and once they'd indulged my eccentric side, everyone was able to guzzle normal birthday cake to their hearts' content...

NEON PINK

I was covering an R.E. lesson with a Year 3/4 class one day. The L.O. (Learning Objective) left for me was for the children to write their own personal, modern-day versions of The Lord's Prayer. They were to work it out in rough first, on whiteboards or scrap paper, then, once it was checked and ok'd, present it in best on coloured paper and decorate around it. All of a sudden, an irrepressible, high-spirited African-Caribbean girl jumped up from her seat and rushed urgently over to me making indecipherable guttural pleas for help...

Presumably out of curiosity, she had sucked up (and swallowed) what must have been the entire contents of a glittery hot pink gel pen – and still had a whole mouthful dripping down her chin. My heart was in my mouth (it looked as if her own was in *hers*!) High drama ensued as she was rushed to First Aid, while I gave the riot act to the rest of the class about the dangers of putting foreign objects in their mouths. The behaviour mentor then returned and promptly launched into reiterating exactly what I had already said!

It turned out the girl was okay, but to make sure, I spoke to her father at Home Time and advised that, although the pens were probably non-toxic, it was worth having the doctor look her over just in case. The staff were very nice about it and said that by 8 years old, she really ought to have known better; a large part of it was just attention-seeking. You never know what a day will bring...

THE CURSE OF THE 'VIRTUAL' TUTANKHAMUN

In the late 1990s, the college where I taught Graphics had technology funding and prided itself on being at the very forefront of the latest developments. A Loughborough University-based virtual reality company with an education focus made contact with us, bringing in some of their headsets for the staff to try on. Today, these things have shrunk to the size of a pair of sunglasses; and there are strong indications that it really is only a matter of a few short years before an interface can be placed into the very brain, enabling such experiences direct. People apparently are *queueing up* to be the recipients of such an advance – rather them than me! – but back at that time, the equipment you had to wear was enormous and very cumbersome indeed: a bulky and quite uncomfortable headset, utility belt-style paraphernalia around your waist and a force-feedback glove through which to gain sensation, plus positioning, in the virtual environment.

Being immersed in this other world – crude, blocky, limited and disorientating as it may have been – nonetheless blew my mind with its potential; and I agreed to work with the company to create an "industry link" in the form of a character development project with my Sixth Form students. We were, in-so-doing, quite literally, the very first college in the U.K. to forge such links with the V.R. industry – it was truly cutting-edge stuff.

I asked my students each to select a well-known character from history – anyone they wanted – then to research their chosen subject thoroughly; and accurately depict the personality's appearance from the front, back, left and right profiles. They were then to use the reference material gathered to produce a high-quality, three-dimensional coloured model which would be photographed from the same four angles; and a separate, panoramic artwork background related to the chosen theme – the agreement being that the company would do the "tech"-side; magically 'knitting' the photos together to create a 3D avatar of each of the students' characters.

The vast majority of the Sixth-Formers took the challenge very seriously, producing some of their best work: we had such characters as Princess Diana, Julius Caesar, Margaret Thatcher, Winston Churchill, Mother Teresa, Neanderthal Man, Jacques Cousteau, Albert Einstein, John Lennon, Charlie Chaplin, Martin Luther-King and Mahatma Gandhi; plus a few rather tenuous fictional examples which had veered off the given brief somewhat – such as Gandalf, Hercules, Thor and even *The Beano's* Dennis The Menace!

The V.R. company were most enthusiastic about the models and photographs that resulted, and asked the college if they might release me for the day to speak along with some of my students' 3D models at the first-ever World Conference on Virtual Reality, which happened in early 1999 at the former Snibston Discovery Centre. The request was granted; but for some reason the formality of the event was never brought to my attention; and its huge significance went totally over my head – I was just chuffed to have a day off work; and turned up at this conference in jeans and a huge, flame-red woollen jumper down to my knees that my old mum had knitted – only to find myself surrounded by impeccably-suited delegates from all over the world! They listened respectfully to my talk but must have thought I was some kind of mad genius... In hindsight it is very funny but at the time I was *mortified* – it was like turning up in a fancy-dress chicken-outfit to a party where no-one else has bothered!

I ended up wrapping up the college's link with the company after three years, as, disappointingly, they were charging quite a fee for their visits; and frankly, in my opinion, were exploiting the talent of our students to the max, while not actually pulling their own weight sufficiently, or delivering their side of the agreement. The maximum I ever saw them achieve was getting one of Princess Diana's arms to raise slightly; and place some of the students' models (non-moving) into a virtual gallery.

My most enduring memories of the project, however, have to be those surrounding one particular model, created by a straight 'A' Graphics student. Using computer software, he was highly skilled at manipulating media to produce the most sumptuous, layered artwork; with highly-original responses to any brief set. His idea to package "Chocolate D.N.A" is one that particularly sticks in my head... A quiet lad, but a consummate professional even at 17, he had the distinction of being the only student I ever awarded 100% in his year-long Personal Study project; he just listened and followed all advice; going on to become Senior Designer in a Midlands-based Graphics company. While this student absolutely excelled in his own field of expertise, where he struggled was in the sphere of accurate observation drawing or 3D model-making. Without the computer, he was really rather exposed, falling significantly short of the others; and I offered to work with him after school to bring his model up to a passable standard.

The character he had chosen to research and develop was

Tutankhamun. We're most of us familiar with the legendary "Curse" of the boy-Pharaoh – but never did I think this would manifest itself in one of my classrooms. That poor lad's project was *plagued* by misfortune from start to finish... He began with a model which was way too tall, constructed out of plasticine. It couldn't support itself and its legs had to be massively reduced, resulting in a stunted-looking figure. But then it was top-heavy and kept falling forward onto its face, lopping off the carefully-sculpted detail again and again. It happened *numerous* times; and the only way he found around it was to give the model huge, more-or-less club-feet in the sandals to counterbalance it.

Most remarkable of all though, was what happened once he painted it. Following the final photography stage, all the students' models were entombed in a padlocked, ground-level cupboard, not to be excavated until the end of their 'A' Level course. I alone held the key. There was nothing out-of-the-ordinary about any of the other models once that cupboard was finally reopened – all except for Tutankhamun.

Even a full year later, the paint on its surface was – still – *soaking wet...*

9:11, GREEN TRAYS AND THE NIT-NURSE

I once worked in a private setting with the luxury of only 15 children in the entire group – in fact over 20 years on, I can still recite the register! You could achieve so much in a class of that size in comparison to a normal state-school average of 27 to 30-plus; the only downside being that because the parents were paying for it – thousands a term – they could be extremely vocal if dissatisfied with this or that; and so, quite rightly, kept you *very* much on your toes. The school didn't adhere all that religiously to the National Curriculum, but the clear aim was for the children to be at least a year ahead, progress-wise, of their state-school counterparts: they most certainly were – and then some...

I never did rest all that easy with the sense of privilege and opportunity money could buy – but on the plus-side, standards were so much markedly higher right across the board, from general levels of pupil attainment (some had read over 100 books by the time they left Foundation 2, still at the age of 5), to the most lavish school plays complete even with ballroom dancing – the scale of everything was such that you couldn't help but marvel at the whole set-up.

It has to be the only school I worked in where it was possible to walk from one end of the building right to the other without opening a single door – because, from the tiniest age up, respect was instilled in children who were trained from the word go to hold them open for any adult.

It's said that everyone remembers exactly where they were and what they were doing when the 9:11 attacks happened back in 2001: I was no exception. Busy with the school routine, we had been sheltered from much of the breaking news inside the building; and at the end of the day, it was customary for one of the Reception classes to join the other for the final carpet-time session. The parallel teacher and I took it in turns to read the story each day, enabling the other to grab a much-needed coffee and perhaps get some marking done. On that occasion, it was my turn to take both classes; when I had finished reading and had released the children to get their coats from the cloakroom, I came out to discover teachers and Nursery Nurses alike huddled, numb with disbelief, around the classroom TV – on which could be seen the catastrophic footage of the Twin Towers collapsing. It was as if they were in a hypnotised fascination, transfixed by the horror and scale of the disaster – having accompanied an American cousin up to the top floor of the World Trade Centre a decade before, it was still a potent memory and I recognised at once what I was witnessing.

You can't really shield anyone from the enormity of a world event such as that, but nonetheless, my instinct to protect the children kicked in; in alarm, I ordered the staff "Switch it off!" – which they promptly did, snapping out of their collective trance. But despite the attempt at censorship, the very next morning, there was a distinct subdued feel to the class. Several of the children made a bee-line for the construction equipment, one saying as he assembled a tall structure, "A big building fell down..." That is simply how they processed and made sense of the trauma at that tiny age. We stopped, mid-P.E. lesson for a school-wide minutes' silence at 11 a.m. – and, memorably, not a single one of those four year-olds broke it by talking.

One particular 4+ child stood out from all the rest in my class. He was a precocious talent, producing rainbow-striped artwork of a standard remarkable for his age, some of which, in its three-dimensionality, even confounded Piaget's linear theory of child development. Again, in Literacy, he demonstrated a fluent reading age several years above his counterparts. Unfortunately, there was very scant parenting at home. His mother and father, while they were by no means unkind, appeared to lack a sufficient nurturing instinct and, by their own admission, had more or less deferred the boy's upbringing to his older sister, who herself was only eight! It had to be brought home to them how inappropriate this was; they vowed to take more of an interest, but in the meantime, the boy had gone on to develop a massively-inflated ego and a will of iron: he would sometimes plant his feet, refusing to enter the classroom, resulting in my having to resort, with the Head's permission, to physically lifting him into it on several occasions. On would go the waterworks whenever his will was defied – it was almost akin to breaking in a young colt!

He also had an obsession with the colour green. The vast majority of the school's compartmentalised, injection-moulded plastic dinner trays were grey in colour, but there was the occasional green one. It was a case of pure chance whether those lining up for lunch, taking the next tray from the top of the pile, would get that colour – but this child simply *had* to have green, and if none were forthcoming, he would happily try to lift the entire metre-high, precariously-balanced pile of trays from the table just to pull out the only green one from the bottom. When such attempts were intercepted and blocked by staff, the boy would throw a screaming tantrum and be inconsolable – but we just couldn't let him win and get away with such behaviour when all the other children were obeying the rules!

He was a charming, likeable little lad in many respects, with the most winning of faces, but his anti-social behaviour was really obnoxious: he had just had things his own way for too long! One day, when a little girl on his table had made some minor mistake in her work, we heard him say aloud in an amused tone, "Perhaps it's because she's got insects in her hair."

"That's a really rude thing to say!" one of the support staff scolded him: "You say sorry at once!" Upon reflection, it occurred to us what an odd remark it was: one of the Nursery Nurses then saw the boy scratch, took him off into an adjoining room to investigate – and found him, quite literally, *crawling* with lice...

I was called in to see; never had I seen a case so extreme: they were clustered thickly on top of one another, in a stomach-churning brown and greyish band over a centimetre wide at the base of his hairline. Of course all the children then had to have nit-letters urging their parents to treat them with a medicated shampoo that evening – then all the staff had to check each other! Mercifully I was louse-free, almost certainly due to my using hair gel, which the others claimed the creatures avoided like the plague...

"HANDS!"

Occasionally as a supply teacher, you just get one of those odd days where nothing seems to make much sense! I got a late booking one morning to work at a local primary school very close to home. It was a grim, rainy day; and the school was down a sloping path below road level. As I was heading in haste towards Reception, my heavy trolley-on-wheels rattling behind me, I slipped and fell. I was unhurt, but my trousers were plastered in mud from a puddle; which was the last thing I needed and hardly made the best impression on the already highly-strung Headteacher, who happened to be an *uncanny* likeness of my next-door neighbour – I literally did a double-take, I was so shaken by the similarity!

I had 39 Year 6 children jammed like sardines into a tiny classroom (a big class, but not the most I ever had – *90* was the record on one baking hot day; I must have gone half-loopy myself, ending up playing the *Eastenders* theme for that Science class on a set of milk-bottles filled with different volumes of water!)

Many of these fancy architects who so cleverly design attractive new schools, with an octagonal Hall at the centre and all the classroom spaces radiating around its exterior like a gigantic bungalow, seem to have some vital logic-cog missing from their brains: so intent are they on making the building beautiful that they overlook crucial ergonomic and anthropometric data relating to the pupils themselves, their sizes and their comfort needs! So you find coat-hooks, for instance, ridiculously high on the wall, where the small ones can barely reach; and room spaces way too small... Children are *not* static creatures – they move – constantly – and that is something which should be a prime consideration when designing any space for them!

Anyway, it came to the time for Assembly and I led the class into the Hall. The Headteacher spent the first ten minutes *screaming* at the top of her voice at the schoolchildren about this grievance and that – it certainly wasn't a happy atmosphere... All of a sudden, she changed tack and said, "Right, we have a performance from a group of girl dancers to watch." The pupils were terrific gymnasts dressed in flowing, colourful saris, doing cartwheels brilliantly in sync with each other – I was really impressed; and as soon as the music ended and the dancers came to a halt, naturally I began clapping to show appreciation.

I very quickly realised I was the *only* person applauding... the Head had simply said, "HANDS!" and silently the entire Hall had raised their palms obediently to the heavens.

One of the regular staff saw my bemusement and surreptitiously whispered, "She's got a 'thing' about noise." It didn't seem to stop *her* shouting the house down; but maybe a stressful OFSTED inspection was due. Yes, that would explain it...

GUY NEWMOUNTAIN: OFSTED CREEP

Around Easter-time in 1998, I had been filling a gap in Teaching with part-time work as a delivery-man for a local Chinese takeaway. I knew my days were numbered in that job, as the numerous road humps in the Stadium Estate were playing havoc with the car's suspension, leading to repeated, costly repairs. So I applied for an Art and Graphics post at a prestigious local Technology College. I didn't get it, but the teacher who did couldn't persuade her current employers to release her from her contract before the end of the academic year; so to cover the gap at this end, a temporary, one-term contract was offered instead to the runner-up candidate – me. On the back of that opportunity, I took a huge risk: now that

I could state my occupation as "Full-time Teacher," I was granted a mortgage and bought my very first house (Halifax didn't do the comprehensive checks they should have and so had no idea the job was just for that one term!)

Little did I know that the college I had joined were on the brink of a long-awaited OFSTED inspection. Naively, I had no idea what a big deal one of those was; and how much terror such impending visits typically strike into the average workforce. I just did my own thing – and as a temp, the focus wasn't really on me anyway.

A highly eminent and distinguished inspector was, nonetheless, due to observe my lessons with the same class twice within the week. I was teaching History of Art to a class of Sixth-Formers; and he was a great fella, very friendly; I got on with him like a house on fire. The nice thing was, he didn't just sit sternly with his clipboard like an ominous presence at the back of the room; he actively *participated* in the lesson, making little contributions here and there. It was almost like team-teaching. The topic I was covering at the time was Impressionism; and the Inspector happened to mention how much he loved the work of Vincent Van Gogh; who is also a personal favourite of mine.

"Do you know," he said aloud to the whole class, "there's the most amazing song, *Vincent,* which is all about Van Gogh... such a beautiful song – I absolutely love the words and the melody."

Right, I thought... any leverage has got to be good here...

That night I went to the Record Library in town, borrowed a set of slides from the University Library and booked the projector for my next observed lesson. Sure enough, there was the Inspector, watching, eagle-eyed, as I registered the students.

"Now, folks," I announced, "to start with, I've got a little slideshow with accompanying music. I want you to listen carefully to the lyrics and give this extraordinary artist the respect he deserves..."

And I hit "play" on the tape recorder, as Vincent's finest examples lit up the screen, slides changing in time with Don McLean's famous track. I glanced over at the Inspector – his eyes were glazed in blissful rapture...

"Oh – and the music," he said afterwards, "nice touch, that – nice touch..."

I'm not proud of it, but there are indeed times for such shameful 'sucking-up...' I wasn't part of the departmental feedback meeting at the end of the week, but was informed later that OFSTED's verdict on me was, "Inspiring teacher: *nail* this man's feet to the floor!" That resulted not only in my contract being made permanent; it also meant I could continue meeting those mortgage repayments and keep my *home* – all of which helped me to reconcile my creepiness considerably...

THEM AND US

Fairly early on in my Teaching career, I had a "rolling" tutor group, which meant they stayed with you as they moved up through the years. I would always dress with a tie for work; not all the staff did – it was down to individual choice, provided you looked smart; but I had some rather extrovert, brightly coloured examples I enjoyed showing off. The students themselves didn't wear uniform, which was a mixed blessing; as although it allowed them that fashion freedom, it also acutely exposed those from less affluent back-grounds who couldn't compete...

One Friday, I felt like being a little more casual, so I came in without wearing a tie. This was instantly picked up on by one of my Year 11 mixed-race tutees. We'd had a fairly chequered history, as, easily angered, she was volatile, fiercely loyal to her own clique of friends and prone to shouting and storming out of lessons and tutor-time; her lack of punctuality or openness to advice a cause for concern. With a less-than-stable home situation, she was one of those students who needed to be treated with kid gloves; any ongoing drama defused very carefully to avoid being drawn into a spiral of rising tension. She would often be found loose around the college avoiding her classes and would need to be coaxed back into them. But she was also a highly unusual character; asking curious questions like, "Do you enjoy the work, sir?" or telling her friend off for trying to extort money from me one Saturday when I bumped into them in town:

"*Don't* – teachers don't earn a lot, you know!"

(Right or wrong, I still gave them 50p each, so I wouldn't look completely stingy.)

Now, there are very, very few teenagers in my experience who show any significant degree of interest in those adults around them: most are 100% focused on themselves, their peer group and their own immediate needs. Socially, despite her academic shortcomings, this student was really quite astute for her age; she was about to become a school-leaver at 16; and while I was struggling to find many positive attributes to add to her reference ("She is an interesting and capable student who has shown a real enthusiasm and drive to get out of the school environment"), we came to an agreement that I would 'big-up' how interested she was in people. "It is my firm conviction that what makes her unusual is her level of curiosity in those around her." I may well have over-emphasised this quality, but I sensed that she rather liked the fact I had identified a characteristic in her which made her stand out from others; and I believe that she knew, despite the fairly frequent bouts of friction between us, that deep down I was OK and did have her interests at heart.

So anyway, on this particular morning, she asked me, "Sir – how come you're not wearing a tie?"

Thinking I'd get her on-side for looking more laid-back and chilled for once, I answered in a light, friendly tone, "Well – come on – it's Friday, isn't it!"

Her response really took me aback: she said simply, "I prefer you in a tie."

I considered this at length afterwards – there is, of course, a very necessary distance between teacher and pupil; wise is the person who recognises and accepts that early on in their career. You're *not* their "mate" and never will be, nor should you try to be – and

I came to the conclusion that the tie is a very visible symbol of that boundary, which, in its own way, was actually rather reassuring to that student!

Last I heard of her, she had been jailed after stealing £150 from the till of the local chip-shop where she worked. But no-one is all bad; she was one of those people far from doomed to a life of petty crime; and I like to think that hopefully she found her focus, discovered her niche in a satisfying vocation, and flourished later on, doing something fulfilling with her life.

THE GHOSTS OF SCHOOL DAYS PAST

It was a very weird feeling indeed when, some five years apart, two separate assignments came in, first to go and teach in a Primary school and then a Middle school, each of which I myself had attended some 30 years previously. What was even stranger was that, of all the classrooms which could have required cover in that sizeable Primary school, the one I was directed to was the very same I myself had been in at the age of nine: I was able to point to the exact desk and tell the class, "I sat *there!*"

The class teacher back then, who is sadly now deceased, had been particularly influential upon me: a forward-thinking Sikh man with a red turban, he was open-minded enough to ask me upon my sudden arrival in the city at an awkward time of year, early November 1975, what *I* wanted to do. "I'd like to draw," I told him. He took me over to a plan-chest in which lay a whole ream of A3 cartridge paper – the largest sheets I had ever seen at that age. And he *forgot* about me.

I couldn't really blame him: this was the "progressive" era when the new-broom Headteacher's attitude was, hey, man, let's knock down the walls and have three adjacent classes in one big room... There were 74 of us and the noise level used to get so high, one of the other teachers would just completely lose his rag, pick up a nuisance child by the throat and literally *throw* him across the room into a bookcase on the other side, where he would slump, dazed with disbelief, to the floor before starting to bawl...

I took that paper, selected animal books from the library, and copied and coloured individual creatures out large, one a day; cheekily taking it upon myself to stick them up in a line along the outer corridor with Blu-Tack. It was Christmas before the teacher finally realised I wasn't participating in normal academic lessons and insisted I join the rest of the class – but by then it was too late. When my Mum and Dad turned up for Parents' Evening, they were astonished to find my artwork running the entire length of that corridor – I had never demonstrated I could draw like that...

That teacher was to have an even further impact: it was he who arranged a coach-trip for the whole class to visit a Sikh Gurdwara – my eyes were like saucers at the mind-blowing blaze of colour in the tapestries: floor-to ceiling depictions of the gods, golden halos of force radiating from their heads: the blue-skinned Krsna, Ganesh with his elephant's head; the multi-armed Lakshmi, Goddess of Wealth, seated in her holy lotus flower, Shiv with his third eye and a fountain pouring from the top of his head – and, most awesome of all, Kali, master of death, with her ominous tongue sticking out... A Sikh priest came onto the stage and introduced us all to the principle of the Five 'K's: when he came to the Kirpan, the curved, single-edged knife carried by all men of the faith, he explained that every Sikh man had to be prepared to "sacrifice" himself for his religion. My only experience of the word was on my favourite TV show, when a mystical Sisterhood had attempted to burn the hero alive on a huge pyre. When we boarded the coach to leave and the register was taken, my little brother was found to be missing. Ten minutes later, he still hadn't turned up, the teachers were going bananas and I was having kittens, convinced he had been sacrificed. As it was, all was well – he had simply got locked in the toilet!

We were then introduced to the wonderful Indian food, sari shops and multi-coloured sweets on Belgrave's Golden Mile…all such powerful, evocative memories: I went on to have several Asian girlfriends, pursued Art and Graphics into Further Education and ultimately, became a teacher myself…

As for the return assignment to my Middle school, well I can't say my years spent there were the happiest days of my life, but the teachers – early, formative figures – became the stuff of legend; to find myself now teaching alongside some of the original staff who were *still* there after all this time, was truly surreal… In whatever job I found myself, I always seemed to need an end in sight to sustain me, even if that was an unspoken decision, made at the start, to stay 'X' number of years – so I take my hat off to any such dedicated people who turn up day in, day out, year in, year out, decade in, *decade* out to the same place of work. How they do it beggars belief; but I imagine for most, shackled by family and breadwinning responsibilities, the spur is necessity rather than job satisfaction.

The friendly Deputy Head who greeted me, now a mellow, grey-haired, benign figure, bordered on *sadistic* back in the 1970's; he had a reputation that he was definitely not to be messed with. Built back then like an immense beanpole, he had sported a black moustache like Oswald Mosely; and thought nothing of walking down corridors, slapping random pupil heads hard out of the way as he passed. I was once in a pit on stage in an after-school rehearsal for the annual school play; a group of us were meant to be the Lost Boys in *Peter Pan*; and one poor lad had broken his leg and had it sticking out in a plaster cast: that teacher walked by and deliberately – I saw it with my own eyes – kicked him in his broken leg, leaving him writhing in agony… Several years later, it had amused me greatly to spot the man attending a Parents' Evening with his wife at a Sixth Form college his daughter attended. He was coming down the stairs as she mentioned, "We must go and see Mrs Smith" – and in a voice like that of a querulous, tearful little boy throwing a temper tantrum, he moaned, "I don't *WANT* to see Mrs Smith!" Here he was now, a more-or-less spent force, delivering an emotive assembly inspired by a group of girls who had been discovered with a bottle of Bacardi they had smuggled in: "Alcohol – is a substance made up of ethanol, plus water: Ethanol alone is a deadly poison. Take away the water, drink that – and it's night-night – you die." And his final slide on the PowerPoint presentation: "Alcohol... has no place... in school."

The teaching day itself passed relatively uneventfully, but wherever I seemed to go in the building, despite certain cosmetic changes and the addition of new blocks, it seemed to conjure up ghosts: it really had been the school of hard knocks. I could recall the pushing and shoving waiting in line for a Mars Bar from the tuck shop at break time; the slope leading to my form room which became so compacted with ice and grey slush, it was as perilous as glass to climb; and looking down from a walkway bridge, I could see below the mud-rack outside the P.E. block, from which, one winter's day, I had neglected to collect my football boots. They had stood outside for a full week, and when the next lesson came, were filled with a thin layer of ice. The P.E. teacher forced me to wear them and run a full cross-country route in -3 degree sleet and fog: a red mist came down over my eyes and I was off school afterwards for over three weeks with pneumonia...

Then there was the Metalwork room where I once had a piece of my work clamped in a vice. The teacher had told me to file it down, saying "all you need is a bit of elbow grease" – and gullibly, at age 12, I had asked him where to find the tin. I noticed the teacher turned his back, probably so I wouldn't see him shuddering with laughter; then I was sent on a wild goose chase, passed around from one Design department teacher to another, until finally they took pity on me; and, in hysterics, told me the whole thing was a wind-up. The episode did later provide me with inspiration for a children's story – so it wasn't all humiliation!

The dining hall brought back potent memories too: it really was crowd-control for the poor little Russian woman on duty managing the queues of pupils outside trying to ram the door; and god help us if a wasp *("Jasper!")* arrived, for it would be antagonised to the point of fury...

There was the sweetest old dinner lady I used to smile at and say hello to each day in the First Year. Just before Christmas, she called me to one side.

"You take this, now," she hissed intensely, pressing a 50p piece discreetly into my hand and closing my fingers, "It's my last day today; I'm retiring;" then, heartbreakingly, "you're the only child who's ever been nice to me..."

That was really a *lot* of money back then; I simply couldn't reconcile being given it – and the following day, when the boiler packed in and we were sent home at lunchtime in 4ft high snow-drifts (those were real winters), I took out that coin and buried it in the snow at the front of the school...

The concertina plastic doors of the English department brought back memories of an inspirational teacher who could, nonetheless, be quite terrifying when he was angry. I clearly recalled the very first day of a new academic year, when, before he arrived at the lesson to teach us, one of the nastier kids used a novelty rubber-stamp he had got hold of to make a path of tiny black footprints up the freshly painted white wall next to his desk. Later, while we had our heads down reading, the boy's vandalism was discovered by that teacher as he patrolled the room.

"Who did that? Was it *you?*" he asked the culprit.

"No," came the sullen response. Yet there was the rubber stamp, the blatant evidence right there on the wooden desktop. The atmos-phere in the room was electric: you could have heard a pin drop as the English teacher picked it up and took the lid off – we all knew he was going to erupt.

"I think you're lying," he whispered menacingly. "Liar...liar... *LIAR!*"

We almost jumped out of our skins. I remember admiring that menacing, whispering build-up so much – the pupil was a truly malicious, unpleasant character anyway.

But most remarkable of all was to find my very own Form Tutor *still* there, in her final year before retirement. She had been a pretty young brunette, with shoulder-length hair and high-heeled knee-boots; now here she was in flat shoes, hair gone white and cut short into a bob... a little old woman, somewhat taken aback to see me now in my forties, with thinning hair... But it was so lovely to see her and reminisce about the lessons she had taught us – and all things considered, I felt honoured to have had the opportunity to go back to the school in a teaching capacity, albeit just for one day.

Around ten years later, I had to get up very early to get my new young Labrador walked before that day's supply booking; I chose the nearest local park for convenience. It was a cold morning, with a very low-hanging mist, clouds of it at waist level even – and all of a sudden, as I neared a circular, open area with a decorative flowerbed at its centre, an elderly lady appeared out of the mist and approached me.

"Excuse me," she asked, "but did you happen to be a pupil at...?"

To my astonishment, she gave the name of my Middle school.

"Yes – yes I was!" I replied.

"You didn't happen to know…?" she went on, giving the name of my Form Tutor.

"Yes – I did!" I answered incredulously. "She used to be so pretty. She never married, you know."

"I know," the old lady responded; and I noticed with surprise that her eyes were full of tears. "I've come from the General Hospital," she continued, "she died an hour ago…"

"Oh – I'm so dreadfully sorry," I said, feeling a genuine loss. "Were you close to her?"

"You could say that," she smiled, sadly – and vanished into the mist. I never saw her again.

How could a random stranger have known the identity of my former school and Form Tutor?

It wasn't until afterwards, when I recounted the story to a friend, that I realised the old woman had had an uncanny resemblance to that Form Tutor herself – in her aged guise…

I've learned not to scoff at the supernatural: who knows? – it's rather nice to think it might actually have *been* her – come to say, in her own way, a final goodbye.

THE GIVING OF LINES

You can call me old-fashioned or mean-spirited if you like, but my favourite choice of punishment for any pupil whose behaviour had annoyed me was to give them lines – I myself very much savoured composing something articulate to fit the crime; reading out the amusing words in front of the whole class at the point they were given out; so that there would be an influential element of peer judgment as well for the obnoxious perpetrator. If they refused to write the lines, they got an after-school detention instead, meaning that their parents would find out what misconduct they had been up to – so in 99% of cases, the lines were grudgingly accepted!

I was never actually that harsh, I didn't dispense outrageous numbers like 500 or 1000 as miscreants often got when I was at school; in fact I think 300 lines was the maximum I ever gave; deep down I felt it was punishment enough that they even engaged with the task and felt their wrists ache a little. I was also fairly lax if I saw pupils using well-known, tried and tested strategies to speed up the task, such as sellotaping five biros together, so writing one line made many – I never stopped them.

But lines have fallen out of favour in recent times. Over the years I had retained just one example of each sentence given out; and joined them up into a half-metre long vertical band, which I had displayed on the wall behind my desk in the Design staffroom – until my Head of Faculty spotted it and asked me to remove it from sight, lest the highly pro-student Principal saw. "It doesn't sound a very happy experience," she warned under her breath. She was right – but it wasn't *meant* to be!

I'll give you some examples of the kind of offences which elicited my lines over the years: looking back I actually think it was quite a lenient punishment in many cases. For instance I had a Year 11 lad say to me one day, "Sir, my dad owns a whorehouse. Sir, are you a member, sir?" Resulting in:

"I will control my tendency to indulge in immature and foul-mouthed outbursts in Mr Newmountain's lesson."

Another Year 10 student's response when asked to name a famous book was, "Your mum's pants." Which led to:

"I must not act like a Neanderthal primitive in the perfect harmony of Mr Guy's carefully-crafted lesson."

There was one day in a Middle school when a known group of musicians came in to perform exclusively for Year 9 in the Hall. Two younger pupils got their heads together in my lesson, audibly forming a plan to "bunk off." I turned my head in time to see them sneaking out of the classroom door; however a back exit enabled me to cut through the Food room and intercept them before they ever reached the gig. The resulting lines were:

"I will listen to the wise and sagely instructions of my experienced educator, Mr Guy; and resist the primal urge to escape from the Art lesson in pursuit of the forbidden thrills of visiting rock bands."

Possibly the nastiest Year 7 pupil I ever taught was a giant for his age; a bully who would use his physicality to work his entire tutor-group up into a frenzy every morning. So disruptive was he to his Form Tutor that when he came to my lesson and played up in a similar way, I sent a letter home endorsed by his Year Head notifying the family that he was expected to sit a one-hour, after school detention. Apparently, when the letter was opened, the boy told his mother that no way would he be attending – until, to her credit, she told him, "You bloody well will..." As a supply teacher, there was no need for me to supervise that session myself, but I chose to, purely for the satisfaction of dictating the full page I had him write. This is just a small extract:

"I am not here to spend my days building a private posse of adolescent believers around myself; intimidating or leading my peers astray with the hustling, gangster-style persona I sometimes choose to adopt. I shall comport myself public-wise in an acceptable fashion, making a dramatic and lasting change in my behaviour; and becoming a responsible, obedient, polite, helpful and hard-working student, aghast even at the very thought of harming a fly. Bad is not, has never been, and never will be, Good. Should I choose to continue confusing the two in this manner, I may find that I wind up joining a very long, sad list of under-achievers who sell out academically; steering myself into poorly-paid, low-level employ-ment with little fun, no spare cash, few prospects for advancement and possibly even jail on the horizon."

Albeit with a plethora of his spelling mistakes, The Year Office loved it; but my last words proved prophetic; just weeks later, that pupil ended up in a secure juvenile unit after he and his accomplice sexually assaulted a Sixth Form girl in a corridor.

In all other cases, though, my lines were given in response to far lower-level misdemeanours, all of which are long forgotten in the mists of time. For your enjoyment, here are a selection of the best:

"I must not tell my fabulous Graphics teacher to shut up, as I may gain much edification from his eloquent words of wisdom."

"I must refrain from bursting my fancy umbrella open and shut, grinning when reprimanded and still attempting to make contact with my peers in the room once I have been sent out."

"As I know that I am the catalyst for much disruption of the classroom atmosphere, I will resolve to mend my ways in avoidance of such severe penalties as this."

"I will learn from bitter experience that ignoring the direct instruc-tions of my benevolent Art teacher Mr Guy will result in punishment of this harsh calibre."

"I must not indulge in amnesiac behaviour when the opportunity to bring the requisite P.E. kit presents itself."

"When in future I am caught out misbehaving in Mr Newmountain's spectacular lesson, I will take responsibility for my actions instead of pointing my finger at the person next to me."

"I will heed advice, as it is unwise to play with a vice when I should be nice."

"If I wish to be treated as a mature adult, I will resist acting like a member of a savage, face-marking tribe."

"I must not behave like an idiot in the Art lesson and counter-mand Mr Newmountain's instructions."

"I will not swear in school as it sets a bad example to the little Year Sixes and I am sorry for shouting at Fazaan because he nearly poked my eye out with a piece of paper."

"I will learn the folly of my ways and never again finger my phone in the majesty of Mr Guy's immortal Art lesson."

"I must not chew up gobs of paper and expel disgusting missiles from my mouth at unsuspecting citizens."

"Unless I wish for further punishment, I will resist the temptation to make foul-mouthed outbursts in the splendour of Mr Newmountain's Graphics lesson."

"I must not engage in disruptive physical combat and waste the precious commodity of paper on cheap aeronautical malpractice."

"I will refrain from tickling female students like a frenzied octopus when I should be in my seat working for Mr Newmountain."

"Under no circumstances will I ever again make slanderous allegations regarding the sexual orientation of my excellent Graphics teacher."

"Purely due to my futile avoidance of the inevitable forces of consequence, I must now learn from harsh experience that the teacher will always have the last laugh."

SPICE-BREAKER

You can never predict a sudden twist in fate; and what might be just around the corner – which is one of the great 'positives' in Teaching when compared to other jobs: there is endless variety!

In the college at which I was working at the start of the new academic year in late August 1999, tutor groups of students just beginning the Sixth Form were preparing for a brand new intake of Sixth Formers from other schools to replace the Year 11 leavers. To welcome the newcomers and to prevent a possible backlash from the regulars, who might feel their home-turf was being invaded, the idea was introduced of a "Sixth Form Icebreaker" day-trip to London. This was a huge and costly undertaking; involving a whole fleet of coaches and a wide variety of locations across London allocated at random to the different tutor-groups. The day was split in half: there were to be *two* different experiences for each class, to maximise the chances of the students being satisfied with at least one or other of their visits.

There was also an element of "mystery tour" about it, with them not finding out their eventual destinations until the very last minute. Old and new students were paired up to help break the ice; and one of the new Sixth formers in each class pulled two strips of paper out of a hat revealing the secret locations for the day. My own new intake turned out to be really rather a nice bunch, made up in the majority of quiet, softly-spoken and well-mannered Asian students, with the occasional high-spirited lively one in the mix.

The first destination to be pulled out of our hat got a rather unfair, lukewarm response: the R.A.F. Museum in Colindale. One or two of the lads expressed excitement, but there were groans from others who clearly weren't interested; however our second destination, Camden Market, happened to be my own favourite stamping-ground; and I was at least able to placate the class with the promise that it was really well-geared to youth-culture, packed with different shops, fashion and food-stalls and offered something for everyone.

Well, down drove all the coaches before they then split off to their different destinations. At the end of the first placement, it was clear the R.A.F Museum had not been a hit, with several of the group muttering under their breath that we'd "drawn the short straw." It didn't seem so bad to me; they'd had a go in a flight simulator and seen several famous wartime aeroplanes; but the hangar was enormous and quite cold; and I guess the subject-matter wasn't everybody's cup of tea. As we arrived at Camden, none of the Sixth-Formers seemed massively enthused, but on the agreement that they synchronised their mobile phones and promised to be back at the coach 15 minutes before the designated leaving time, I let them loose to go and explore the market independently.

I was waiting at the coach as they all straggled back several hours later: my distinct impression was that, while it had been ok for them as an experience, it was certainly nothing to write home about.

All of a sudden, from across the road, up went an excited shriek: "Sir! Sir!"

I swung around to see one of the new intake waving frantically in my direction. "What is it?" I called.

"OMG Sir – *The Spice Girls* are here! Please, can we wait and see them – please?"

Who would have thought it? From what looked like being judged a rather unremarkable damp squib of an outing, I couldn't believe our luck. Admittedly, The Spice Girls were no longer in their "Zig-a-zig-ah" *Wannabe* heyday by then, but they were still scoring Number 1 singles.

Fortunately, we had an accommodating driver who agreed to wait a while longer. It turned out that the group (who by that time had famously fired guru Simon Fuller and were managing themselves) had arranged for the Camden branch of Footlocker to be temporarily closed while they made an impromptu shopping spree for new pumps. Ginger (Geri Halliwell) had already parted company with the rest by then, but sure enough, out spilled Posh (Victoria Beckham) wearing khaki combat trousers, Sporty (Mel C) and Scary (Mel B), much *smaller* than life, but to the infinite delight of my tutor-group. Instinctively, as Baby Spice passed by, I extended my arm and said "Hello, Emma!" – and rather graciously, Miss Bunton smiled sweetly and shook my hand. It *made* the day for my students...

At a motorway service-station halfway back up the M1, all the coaches stopped for a scheduled break – it's no exaggeration to say the other students were *green* with envy when they heard my tutor group's news: their street-cred went through the roof! And when I told our formidable college principal, who was poised on the tarmac back at college to oversee the Sixth-Formers' return, it put a beaming smile on her face too – so, indirectly, it didn't do mine any harm either...

THE LOATHED LESSON

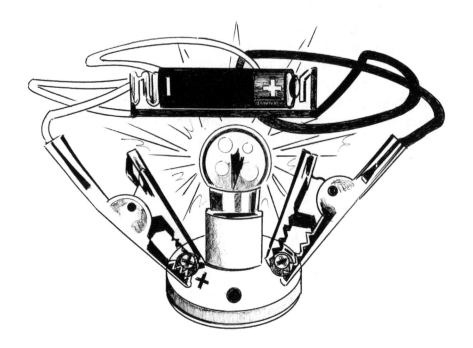

Of all the Primary school lessons I was most reluctant to deliver as a supply, it had to be Circuits. I seemed to have to teach that all the time. Somehow the Science departments never seemed to be ready for the topic: they probably hated it too and so decided to palm it off on unwitting supply teachers. It was invariably sprung on me at the last minute; and on virtually every occasion, I couldn't rely on pupils to be sufficiently competent on my behalf; and would need to sacrifice my whole lunchtime to disentangle the mass of crocodile clips and wires from each other, many of which would not have been touched or tested for a year. As if that wasn't enough, half the bulbs would be broken or the batteries dead, so that even when the earnest, excited pupils had listened carefully to instructions and assembled their circuits correctly, their attempts to get the required results would be frustrated by faults in the equipment. Detective work was then required to identify exactly what wasn't working; and in the classroom I would find myself in demand in seven places at once, with only two hands to lend!

The scarcity of functioning bulbs meant that often they would be poached from any group of pupils lucky enough to have them by those from another table, leading to fights, whining and tears. It would all evoke memories of a fantastic Secondary school teacher, one of the sole staff who could occupy the most challenging students in the school: he would keep their attention only with the most radical experiments, such as dissecting a pig's head in front of them or getting each of them to stand in a bucket of water as a mild electrical current was passed from one of their bodies through the others... all of which they loved.

To cap it all, I myself seemed to have a mental block about the symbols and jargon used, forgetting it from year to year: conductors, insulators, closed and open electrical circuits, components, motors, buzzers – the whole lot made me switch off (get it?) completely; and I would have to clue up again as best I could just minutes before the class came through the door! Now obviously it's important that children experience the process of conducting investigations by themselves; and while I was all for that and understood the need for it, sometimes time constraints dictated a different approach. Over the years I became more wily: if they're going to dump this lesson on me and leave me to teach it, I'm damn well going to go about it my own way!

So I would gather together a model set of all the best-functioning bulbs, batteries, motors and wires, get the children to write all the theory work first, then create a blank table for results to go in – and then, teacher-led, with of course, the assistance of eager pupils, I would conduct each required experiment from the front. Collectively the class would interpret and agree the results; and then each individual pupil wrote them up to fill in their own table. It meant that any time remaining could be used for their own experimentation and play – but at least that way, we had the precious results and conclusion out of the way!

A GUILTY CONSCIENCE

I had no real justification to do what I did in this instance, but at the time, I was quite low; and state of mind was undoubtedly a contributory factor. I had recently handed in my notice at a school, having secured a new post elsewhere; and it was the end of an era, leaving me feeling uncertain as to what exactly the future was going to hold.

Whilst clearing out my belongings from the walk-in cupboard on the penultimate day before handing back my keys, I came across a sealed A1 pack of coloured tissue paper standing upright behind the door. I had ordered it for the pupils at the start of the academic year from the usual stationery catalogue, but it was surplus stock they'd not got around to using. I took the pack home that night and wrapped a hand-made leaving card for each of my many favourite colleagues in a sheet of coloured tissue paper. The vast majority of it, however, stood unused for years, gathering dust behind my dog's basket.

It was the school's, yet remained at my home when it didn't belong to me; and the shame of having it ate away at me: in my head, the act was magnified into something terrible. I even confessed it to an ex-colleague when I visited her years later. What I actually sought was her criticism – it would have made me feel better somehow to be scolded – but her smiling response was, "I think after the years you gave us, Guy, you're entitled to a pack of tissue paper – don't you?"

I knew I wasn't – I should have taken it back.

Coincidentally, almost a decade later, I got an opportunity to salve my conscience. An assignment came up back at the school and I approached the stock-taking technician when no-one else was around.

"I feel really bad; I've had this at home and meant to bring it back in for some time!" I said, passing over the A1 pack with genuine relief.

It stopped short of a full confession, but in the moment, was the closest I could muster.

"Another one seeking absolution!" she joked, relieving me from the parcel's weight – along with a sizeable burden of guilt.

DIFFERENCES IN OUTLOOK

In the same class, I once taught Graphics to two profoundly deaf girls, each of whom were talented artists. While not without its challenges, it was a most interesting and rewarding experience to teach them. Each girl struggled to speak clearly, which certainly had an impact on their self-esteem; but they were supported greatly in all their lessons by the presence of a highly-dedicated signing teacher from the college's Hearing Impaired Unit; a woman who was most keen to secure the girls' understanding of the learning covered in each lesson; and what they needed to achieve from week to week.

She would come to see me frequently between sessions and would take notes from our conversations to ensure she herself could pass on to the students exactly what I needed them to do.

Inevitably, the pace at which the girls worked and the demands from other subjects meant that they did fall behind the rest of the class somewhat, but via extra input and clear, explanatory, written instructions leaving nothing to chance, we saw to it that by the end of the year, they had accomplished enough of the key coursework tasks to guarantee a more than decent grade at GCSE. Each of the girls went on to pursue Art and Design at GNVQ level into the Sixth Form; however, while they had both held things together admirably up to that point, their attitudes began to diverge dramatically...

One of the two students had the loveliest outlook: always with a smile, she was popular, receptive, willing and so very positive about every creative task set – it was truly a joy to teach her throughout all her four years at the college. I even bumped into her a couple of times in town years later whilst taking a short cut through a fast-food restaurant to a local shopping centre; and on both occasions, she beamed and waved animatedly in delight. That girl went on to be one of the runner-up supermodels in a televised Reality TV series; she is highly active on social media and has recently opened a stylish hair and beauty salon of her very own with her boyfriend, already visited by a number of celebrities.

The *other* deaf girl, while relatively easy to motivate up to the point of her GCSE's, became increasingly surly, resistant to instruction and almost impossible to deal with at times. I remember meeting her mother once at a Parents' Evening; and I'm afraid to say I didn't warm to her one bit. If I recall correctly, the woman had a fairly high-profile job in the public eye; in Media of some kind; and while she could be highly strident and vocal on her daughter's behalf, at every opportunity going all-out to make sure the college staff had put sufficient strategies in place to support her child; she herself seemed to resent the demands her daughter put on her time, viewing her almost as an encumbrance! That may not be true, but is definitely the impression I was left with – and I strongly believe the girl picked up on that sense of being resented, which may well have coloured her own behaviour.

While never particularly cheery before, she developed a permanent scowl on her face; and her entire body language gave off hostility and resentment: she would *physically* cold-shoulder you

187

away. It was nothing personal; she seemed to rotate her hatred of the staff periodically between us: one day you'd be flavour of the month; the next she couldn't stand you!

Again, years later, I saw her once on the High Street in town, her face plastered in make-up to an almost excessive degree; and sadly, I was later informed that she had reached such a bad place, she ended up in the most notorious of local mental asylums – long since demolished.

How curious it is that two students who started out with more-or-less the same basic disability should go on to have such opposing paths and fortunes in life. I don't believe the way for the more successful girl was made especially easier by anyone in particular, or that she was from any more markedly affluent background; but her personality is by far her greatest asset: she has overcome real adversity to achieve what she has; and I could not be more happy and proud for her.

It's true I have no idea what other hurdles life may have thrown in the way of the more troubled girl; but I can only hope she went on to gain greater peace of mind with the passing of time.

SANTA GUY

I lost count of the number of times I was invited to dress up and be Father Christmas for the day in various Infant schools; there must have been at least five or six appearances in different settings. The job was not without its hazards: so fired up and excited was I after the first successful performance that I braked too late on the journey home and drove my little car straight into the back of a large van.

Luckily no-one was injured, but it was a costly reminder not to get carried away...

On one occasion, I was asked to stay in character after Assembly had finished, so that parents could bring their children up to be photographed with Santa. They did provide me with a chair to sit on, but the problem was, I could barely see a thing behind the heavy cotton-wool beard and overhanging hood. Up stepped a proud young Asian mum and, before I knew it, she had suddenly plonked a 3-month old baby onto my chest. Wearing the huge, padded mittens which were part of the outfit, I couldn't get a secure grip on the precious bundle; and to my alarm, felt the infant sliding steadily away – fortunately someone came and rescued her just before she dropped out of my lap onto the floor!

One time I thought I would make a very slow, silent entrance using a measured policeman's stride to suggest that Santa was extremely old: the expectant children could see my solemn approach from a long way off down a narrow corridor; it must have taken a full five minutes for me to actually reach the front of the Hall. The red robe was extremely long on that occasion, resulting in my feet being completely hidden. Unfortunately, the inexorable "glide" effect that resulted absolutely terrified one small Nursery child, who had to be taken out. Somehow, being hidden behind the costume gives you dramatic license to be much larger than life; I was able to be outra-geously cheeky to the various Headteachers, much to the children's delight; and could make up outlandish stories to my heart's content:

"I was in my grotto meeting some children last week and I asked one very mischievous little child how old he was and he said 29! So then I said, well if you're really 29, then you're grown up and you don't need presents! And well, he didn't like that one bit, so then he told me how old he really was – and do you know how old he was? He was *five!*"

One especially awkward moment occurred when the lively son of a Teaching Assistant came up close and worked out my true identity from the trademark cowboy boots he spotted sticking out from under the coat.

"It's Mr Guy!" he cried. "I know who you are – you're Mr Guy aren't you?"

I had to pretend jovial surprise.

"Mr Guy? Whoever's *that?*" I answered in a Captain Birds Eye voice. He just wouldn't go away and I was in a dilemma whether to burst his bubble forever and admit it, or keep up the pretence: it was all I could do to stop the lad trying to pull the flaming beard off, but I couldn't very well reprimand him, as he was the son of a colleague who clearly found my predicament hilarious!

The following year I brought in wellies as a disguise to prevent being rumbled a second time... On that occasion, Santa had to judge a Christmas tree-making competition. There they were at the front: a stunning, powder-snow covered, icicled array, from the most enormous right down to the tiniest, which I had secretly helped the (then) object of my desire to construct for her class. She was so keen to win the competition, but given my input, it seemed as if that would somehow be cheating: by way of a compromise, I gave her tree third prize – but I still felt very guilty...

The last time I took on the role, I decided to be a Dancing Santa. The performance was inspired by those foot-tall mechanical festive figures which both play and respond to music: you know, first one begins dancing, then it triggers the second, and that one finally activates the third.

Into the Hall I plunged, a real sensation, kicking one leg up ridiculously after the other as if I was doing the Russian Polka. I'd even located a set of battery-operated Christmas lights to insert through the costume to simulate the aurora borealis. An aisle had been created for me to walk up, but, as always has to be the case, one pupil, sitting cross-legged, was unexpectedly sticking way out into it – I only narrowly averted a collision with him which nearly sent me flying, not to mention potentially landing on the other children – but luckily I managed to regain my balance; and at least the other staff were still chuckling about my "unusual interpretation" over their breaktime coffees.

THE SCRUNCHED-UP BALL OF PAPER LESSON

I can't recall the exact details now, but there was a very weird routine I once encountered during a fantastic Middle school maternity cover: mid-term and actually, mid-lesson, old Art & Design groups would suddenly come back to write an assessment on the module they had done previously in that subject; then the current group would rotate to a different discipline. In any event, I was thoroughly confused by proceedings and found myself unexpectedly faced with unfamiliar pupils anticipating a new module. *If* the departmental management had in fact forewarned me, which they may well have, the actual way their system operated had gone completely over my head; so much so that when the new group turned up, I wouldn't accept them and returned them to their previous teacher thinking there had been a mistake! There was a knock-on effect, as other groups then also got sent back to their earlier groups!

I had thrown a real spanner in the works – it was a complicated mix-up; and when the mess was finally understood by the Head of Department, the penny dropped that I did indeed have a new group about to arrive, with no work ready for them. I had to ad-lib; it was a case of really thinking on the spot. I began trawling through the absent teacher's work pack to find something suitable for a launch lesson, but to no avail. I could feel myself starting to panic; some sheet on the desk was clearly of no relevance and automatically, I crushed it into a ball to throw in the bin. And all of a sudden, there was the solution, staring me in the face... *The Scrunched-Up Ball of Paper Lesson!*

It was the perfect introduction to observation drawing: quite a tricky challenge, but a short lesson absolutely complete in itself which would allow me to catch my breath and plan for subsequent meetings with the group. There was no need to get out other equipment; all the pupils needed was a pencil. I got them all to write the title at the top of a blank page, then gave them each a sheet of blank newsprint. On a countdown from 10 to zero, they all excitedly smashed their page into a tight bundle, the rule being that they could rotate it on the table top to a position of their choosing, but that once their hand left the object, they were not permitted to move it again.

We actually got some wonderful sensitive studies out of that chaotic beginning, every "scrunch" absolutely unique; and the lesson became an invaluable staple in my collection of back-up resources.

FACING MY OWN FEAR

I have a lifelong, morbid terror of wasps. There's no logic to a phobia; where exactly it stems from I have no idea. Perhaps as a tiny pram-bound baby I had a traumatising close encounter with one – who knows – but if you've ever seen the face of *Vespula vulgaris* enlarged, it is a hairy, alien-eyed, serrated-jawed mask of utter evil... There's something about their bad temper and aggression, their persistence, their steadfast refusal to go away, their droning buzz far deeper than the rest of the insect world, the weight of their swollen, venom-dripping abdomens hanging pendulously below them – and of course, knowledge of the sting; its alkaline poison the source of excruciating pain...

So attuned to them am I, I can tell within a nano-second if one is around; I would never dream of harming any other animal, but they are the one creature for which I have no mercy: any wasp that enters my home has signed its own death-warrant... Only the queens survive the winter, which means the first ones of the year (any you see from late March to mid-May) are all royals; and It's actually a very misguided kindness to set them free; because from one released queen can come a nest of up to 70,000 – causing (via pest-control exterminators) an infinitely higher death-toll because of your initial softness...

But in the presence of tiny children, you, the teacher, are the adult and you *must* look confident! As even *Dr. Who* (my lifelong hero) once said, courage isn't just a matter of not being frightened, it's being afraid and doing what you have to anyway. You can't let the kids see your fear, or your hang-ups may be passed on to them; and if they are already scared, then it's necessary to show mastery of the situation.

Two particular instances come to mind when I've had to fake such fearlessness. The first, believe it or not, was in the Deep South of Mississippi, during a scorching summer in 1991. I had gone out via Camp America to be Art Director at Henry S. Jacob's Camp, unaware that, as well as copperheads and diamondback rattlesnakes being rife on the site, the beams on the forecourt outside the wooden Art and Crafts cabin were a haven for some *three* different species of wasp! Someone up there must have it in for me, I thought, raising my head in disbelief to the heavens. Is this your idea of punishment? You could even spot the upturned paper-cup nests hanging down as the Potter wasps milled around them, but there were also the weirdest Ichneumon species whose abdomens hung by the flimsiest strings and seemed barely attached to the rest of them. And these were big insects, in a different league altogether from the common UK wasp. 99 percent of the time they went about their business causing no bother to anyone, but then there were other days when, inexplicably, one after another, they seemed to take it into their heads to leave the nest and dive-bomb their way into the classroom itself!

195

The five and six-year-olds drawing, painting or candle-making inside the studio would scream, "Guyyyy!" and even stronger than my own terror was the instinct to protect them. Mercifully, the room was equipped with plentiful cans of fly spray; I would grab one of these and squirt away for dear life. Never had I seen such powerful projectile jets in an aerosol: they would literally slam the wasps against the windows – but that force was needed: so strong were these creatures that they would get up again and yet again before finally succumbing... It felt like a scene out of *Alien* – but somehow we got through the summer and lived to tell the tale.

The *other* incident happened right here in a local primary school classroom. It was an ice-cold winter's day at the very start of the spring term, and, having only just sent my Year 2 class off from the carpet input session to work on a task, my attention was drawn to a jostling commotion at one of the desks, with children shouting excitedly; pushing, shoving and shouldering each other out of the way to gain a better view of... something. I parted the crowd only to see them focused intently on one of the wooden crayon containers in the centre of the desk – in which crouched the most colossal queen wasp, sluggish from the cold and clearly woken prematurely from its hibernation. One by one the children were actually *squeezing* it – I doubt they had ever seen a wasp close-up before or realised the danger – it was simply a moving, living novelty and the source of the greatest curiosity! *How* none of them got stung I will never know – but I dove in there and snatched the container up just in time – the entire class would have descended into high drama had one of them been impaled!

Once things had calmed down, it actually proved a valuable learning opportunity for the group; we went on to discuss wasp safety, how best to behave if ever approached by one, their nest-building skills with paper engineering, how they can walk on water and the positives of having them in the food chain to keep pest numbers down. But little did the class know how much I'd had to man up to deal with the incident – and, deep down, how freaked out I was!

SECTIONAL VIEWS

A particularly Low Ability Year 11 population were struggling to focus on the theory element of their Graphics GCSE course; in particular, Working Drawings and Drawing Systems. I decided that perhaps a more hands-on, practical approach may help them to understand the concepts. The next upcoming challenge was for them to master Sectional Views; and I was at a loss to find an inexpensive simple object in sufficient number for a whole year-group to cut through. It just so happened that the following weekend, I was walking my dog in the local park and came across a patch of freshly fallen crab apples under a tree. Like a bolt of lightning, inspiration struck. What could be a better subject for Sectional Views? Bitter, so they couldn't be scoffed during lesson time, easily cut through with a safe, rounded, non-sharp breakfast-knife, the simplest structure for the students to copy on the inside; and best of all, they wouldn't cost a thing! To the bemusement of passers-by, I began excitedly ramming my coat pockets full of the best specimens until I had collected enough tiny apples for 75 students (all three classes); going on to secure the loan of a set of knives and plates from the college canteen the following morning.

While the actual drawing exercise itself presented a successful, achievable challenge, what I hadn't counted on was the students pelting the apples onto the floor in disgust after trying them and finding them way too sour. I passed a bin bag around of course at the end of each lesson to collect the remnants visible on the desktops, but didn't discover the mess on the floor until the end of the morning. I just didn't have time or frankly the inclination to go around the room cleaning up after them.

I can still hear the elderly pint-sized little school cleaner protesting to her friend in astonishment at the end of the day, "What's been going on in here? There's all these little *apples!*"

The Mock Exam followed a few weeks later; and as much to amuse myself as to help the students revisit that learning, I added a drawing with the taunting words:

"Hooray! – this *delicious* sandwich has been freshly made for you. Draw a neat sectional view through it showing two layers of cheese and one of tomato between the slices of bread."

Eventually, I got the papers back to mark, curious to see how the Year 11's had responded. My most notoriously defiant student had scored a wobbly line through "delicious," replacing it with the most cutting judgment he could muster: the single, blotchy, ink-stained retort: "mongey..."

THE DEADLY ROCK-BACK

I was in the middle of a two-week stint teaching a lovely class of Year 1/2 children, with the teacher off for unspecified reasons; although I did gather, via the clandestine, hushed remarks of other staff that "extreme exhaustion" post-OFSTED inspection was the probable cause... One notable member of the class was a 6 or 7 year-old severely autistic boy rarely able to focus or engage in lessons. He had 1:1 provision for most, *but* (and this is the key thing!) not all, of the day... I did have some measure of experience with autistic children, but right from Day 1 of this assignment, I had vocalised my concerns about the fact that, although there was a designated carpet space and mat for him, there were unsupervised spells when the pupil in question was effectively 'loose' around the edges of the classroom with no supervision, more or less doing his own thing; which involved pulling the lids off markers or rolling various small classroom objects around on the work surfaces.

Many of these were potential choking hazards and often they would enter his mouth; however I was told this was absolutely standard behaviour for him and that in fact he almost needed to be given that degree of free rein to move about independently. I had, in truth seen such behaviour before with autistic children; in certain cases, there seems to be an all-consuming need to negotiate the very periphery and boundary of whatever environment they enter; they will often head straight for the windows.

It did become increasingly clear as the days went by that this specific boy also exhibited a growing defiance, resisting the instructions of his different carers and screaming if thwarted in his attempts to accomplish something which was often dangerous. This morning the defiance had manifested itself in his repeatedly rocking backwards on two legs of his chair the classic hazardous way; and ignoring instructions from his 1:1 to stop.

11.30 came and the lady in question informed me that she was going as usual for her lunch break; I was whole-class teaching at this time, modelling number-formation on the whiteboard at the front of the room, when, within seconds, there was a crashing sound... I looked up in time to see the tail-end of the autistic boy's flight backwards as the last two ground-based legs of his chair finally gave way; the back of his head meeting the hard, unyielding ridges of an old-fashioned radiator, from which he then slid down on all fours onto a woolly green carpet.

"WhoOops!" I said in a cheery, upbeat tone, going over to help the lad to his feet, comforting arm on his shoulder (despite the wisdom of the zero-physical contact policy, if you are in any way a human being at such times, you offer a measure of comfort, especially with tiny children); always my stance to try and defuse the magnitude of these things before tears set in. Usually those tears are more an outlet for wounded pride than the pain of the injury – but not this time...

As he rose to his feet, I found my own hand and arm literally drenched in blood, a deep, dripping gash to the back of his head, and the scariest thing of all, no crying whatsoever... As I was informed later on, apparently, there are very few nerves in that area; but for all I knew, he had sustained serious brain damage!

Now imagine you are on your own in that scenario, in a classroom full of vulnerable children, one of whom is in a real emergency situation; the injury is beyond classroom containment and no-one is around to help. No phone in the room, no adjacent classrooms within sufficiently quick reach. The cardinal rule of course is never – *ever* – to leave a class unattended – it is certainly a "sackable" offence for a supply teacher. I heard, for instance, of one naive soul who chose to leave a classroom prematurely simply to get his timesheet signed for his agency – that, understandably, was sufficient to get him the boot. The choice of which action to take is a judgment call only you can make in that moment – I felt I absolutely had to act; there was no time even to issue instructions to the rest – I ushered the wounded boy into the empty corridor and shouted for help from the doorway – which fortunately was only seconds in arriving; two first-aiders rushing to the rescue.

The boy's mother was called in (showing astonishingly scant concern for his welfare) and the requisite incident slip and bumped-head letter issued to her. Mercifully, no misfortune befell the remainder of the class who were completely on their own for half a minute – it could have, easily: such things can happen in a split second; and had it done so, quite aside from the awfulness of any other child being injured, I would have been left utterly exposed to allegations of negligence. Despite assurances from support staff that no such action was necessary, I felt it important to immediately seek out the Headteacher and explain the situation, offering to make a written note of exactly what had occurred, which the school could keep on file – she acknowledged it was a good idea. An extremely level-headed person, her only remark was, "They're told all the time not to rock back on their chairs..."

In all my years of classroom teaching, never before was a child in my charge injured like that, so it was actually quite upsetting for me; and of course as the teacher, you still have the remainder of the day to get through!

I would urge anyone who finds themselves in a similar type situation to record *everything*, sign and date the document and keep a copy for yourself as well as for the school!

The most serious dimension here, however, is that there *used* to be provision for this autistic boy after 11.30 a.m. up until lunchtime – there no longer is. If a child as severely compromised as that is going to be integrated into mainstream school, the emphasis being on the policy of "inclusion," then he or she needs that degree of 1:1 support *every minute of the day*: what happened is a perfect illustration of that need. The fault is not at the level of the individual school – it is a governmental one for withdrawing the necessary funding.

Once I had informed my agent of the incident, she did advise that I formally ask for that full 1:1 provision, whether or not the request be granted (and it was not); and to insist that the school at very least *record* the fact I had requested it. That in turn ensured a paper trail existed – as much for my own protection as the child's.

BEWARE THE NURSERY NURSE...

Never cross or underestimate the ferocity of a Nursery Nurse; they can be highly militant, have their own union; and where there are several in the same setting, act as a single entity: upset one and you upset 'em all. Many are brilliant classroom managers; but an equal number suffer from the delusion that they are actually teachers and have a much larger than life, domineering manner to match.

In a private setting, I was obliged to have one in my 4+ class who had been there since the days when nuns ran the school.

She had worked for a decade-and-a-half with an ageing woman teacher who was winding down in her career; a kindly lady who had happily delegated more and more duties and power to her, giving her delusions of grandeur and a massively inflated ego – and I, newly-appointed to be not only that beloved elderly teacher's young successor, but also a *fella*, could do nothing right in her eyes. Her whole body language made it clear how outraged she felt at my presence.

She cornered me on Day One, minutes before the class were due to come through the door for the very first time, demanding, "What do you see as my role?"

"Well, to be honest, support!" I replied.

To which she echoed in disgust, "Support..."

She truly believed she was a teacher. She would purposely undermine me, boom everything she said, seize control of whole-class activities that were not her remit and confuse the children as to who, in fact, was in charge. There were times I couldn't get a word in edgeways in the classroom.

Exasperated, I would mention the various goings-on to my lovely retired next-door neighbour, herself an ex-teacher; and she would warn me, "You've got to show her who's boss..."

My best friend was less polite.

"You should put her in her place!" he urged. "Use that line from *The League of Gentlemen*. Shout her surname and tell her: "There are *ARSES* need wiping"!"

I tried everything, bought flowers for her on her birthday, had all the children sign a class card for her – nothing worked: with her gunshot voice, she tried to dominate everything. And that, to me, rather than conveying confidence, is the behaviour of someone who is *desperately* insecure...

It took a lot of guts from me to confront this particular individual, but in the end I had to – I was sitting on too much pent-up resent-ment. Well aware that our department was not gelling as intended, the Head insisted on us having an urgent impromptu meeting, which I unashamedly seized control of; I cited many examples of the woman's non-co-operation, which was no secret to the other staff: they themselves had witnessed it and were equally bewildered by her attitude.

"Frankly, what on *Earth* do you think you are doing?" I asked her outright. "You're *not* a teacher. You want to be a teacher? Go and do a teacher training."

Cornered, the Nursery Nurse lost her temper and tried to defend her behaviour, claiming I had made her feel "one inch tall" when I replaced the dog-eared, reused drawer labels she'd put up with my own individual artwork; but I had too many examples of her misconduct to voice in response: she was bang to rights and my co-teacher had my back.

I did finally get an apology, a grudging handshake and a promise from her to get back on the Valium – but within a term, she rose up again.

Her favourite ruse to escape a day's work was to claim her daughter in Year 6 had just vomited and had to be taken home. This excuse she used on no less than three occasions, giving an identical – gruesome – description in each case: "She's really *crusteh*..." I was only too happy to let the woman go for the day – the class was transformed in her absence!

The best way to rise above someone so unpleasant and uncooperative – is to quietly demonstrate excellence in your own sphere. I did this via our Class Assembly for The Queen's Golden Jubilee; spending weeks preparing sets and a self-written script: the Nursery Nurse failed to do the majority of tasks assigned to her (I suspect having been drinking the night before, but also, almost certainly, in an attempt to disrupt proceedings). After overwhelming applause from the delighted, cam-cording parents, she had the front to whisper in an aggrieved tone to an after-school colleague, "He took all the credit..."

Ultimately, she became a threat to my leadership; I took down her name-card from my door and had her removed from the class by the Head. Even then, she found spurious grounds to re-enter the room whenever she could.

I could have stayed in the job, which was a very cushy number indeed; fabulously paid, way above the Teacher's Pay Scale – but life is too short: every day would have been a fight – and you should never stay in a job just for the money. So, making an excuse that I had paid off my mortgage and was going on a (non-existent) trip around the world, I handed in my notice. But she was the reason.

When asked what I would like as a parting gift, I cheekily requested a laminator, but the school wouldn't stretch to that. Ironically, it was this same Nursery Nurse who was dispatched to a garden centre to collect something for me. She picked a floral plant tub containing one final, covert jibe: a purple china *toadstool*. I didn't dignify her behaviour with a farewell.

In my mind's eye, I can still see her huge, slab-like grey toes and cracked heels that were out on display in her sandals every day.

And – unbelievably – 20 years on, she is *still* there...

TEMPUS FUGIT

Occasionally, at the start of the school day, I would be waiting at the traffic lights to turn right towards the college, while a myriad of my GCSE students milled over the crossing, carrying their A3 plastic Graphics folders in an assortment of translucent gel colours. I would think, incredulously, they're bringing that work for *me*... for my lesson... I never stopped being grateful for that; just for the fact that I had been sufficiently effective at what I did to motivate my students in a forward direction.

And at other times, at the end of school, whilst walking to my car through a leafy churchyard, I might overhear my name being mentioned: "Mr Guy!" – or, once or twice a child whispering to her mother, "That's my favourite teacher..." Moments like that you want to hold onto *forever*; they always cheer your heart...

But one day, an amazing thing happened which had never occurred before; sobering, yet pleasing in equal measure. A little Year 1 girl I had taught the previous day came in the following morning and said to me with excitement, "Mr Guy, you were my *MUM'S* teacher!" It turned out to be true: 20 years earlier I had indeed taught her mother GCSE Graphics back when she was a 14-year-old in Year 10. Two generations... It seriously brought home to me how long I had been at this teaching thing. Actually, I was very happy about it – but I did throw in the towel before any child ever came in and said, "You were my GRAN's teacher!"

TEACHING AN ADULT TO READ

Part and parcel of being a teacher is that you never – really – retire. It's rather similar to a doctor finding that, outside of work, friends and family will always seek advice for this and that form of ailment!

In the idyllic cul-de-sac where I used to live in better days, each of us neighbours would take it in turns to host a Christmas get-together ("Guy's Neighbourhood Social" I called mine); and such conversations would frequently arise at these parties. Most Education-based chat would centre around one or other of the guests remarking that they could never do what I did; as no way would they put up with disruptive behaviour and would "throttle the little b******s." Although I certainly felt like doing that once or twice, I would usually counter the negative opinions by arguing nobly with the speaker that, if you give up on students like that, what you miss out on is seeing them eventually begin to respond and turn completely around – which is incredibly rewarding. The snorts of derision were audible – I don't think I swayed any of the old folk much!

Anyway, at one such gathering, while the chat was in full flow, a softly-spoken 42 year-old Asian man who lived on the opposite side of the close turned to me and said in a hushed, secretive tone, "You know, Guy, I never learned to read – they said I am dyslexic..."

It was unquestionably a plea for help; how else could I interpret that? The problem was, as a supply teacher, I was no longer attached to any specific school; and had no idea what was available in terms of Adult Literacy materials – or where to get them. What I *did* have was an Early Years reading scheme: a full set of 120 picture-books which I had salvaged from being chucked out by one school for being outdated: I knew the scheme yielded success; the only problem was, the subject-matter itself was entirely geared to teach 4+ age children.

"Look," I said to him, "I can't make you any promises at all. A lot is going to depend on you and how willing you are to engage with material which you're definitely going to find beneath you... *but* if you're prepared to swallow that; and come for a lesson *every* weekday evening at 6pm, I won't charge you a penny and we can give it a shot – what do you reckon?"

He virtually bit my arm off; to his credit the fella was true to his word and came over for a lesson every night for six months.

The first pre-reader books in the set were incredibly basic: "red", "ball", "door", "a red ball", "a red door", etc. but the scheme was nonetheless sound, with each book building on previous knowledge.

I would print out as flashcards all the vocabulary the man would need to master the next book, and would only lend it to him once he knew all the words in it. That way, success was more or less guaranteed. Parallel to the flashcards, which just had to be recognised as a whole, I taught him individual phonics, trained him to blend them together by sounding out the individual letters; and to recognise different consonant clusters.

The poor guy wasn't dyslexic at all! The only real problem had been a couple of bad teachers who had damaged his confidence when he was young – he had seized up and felt forever incapable of learning to read.

Gradually the books progressed from small phrases to full sentences; from sentences to paragraphs – and from paragraphs to full pages. I'm not saying it was plain sailing all the way – there was a heart-stopping moment almost at the very end of the scheme when the neighbour seemed to forget everything: it appeared all he had learned had just – evaporated – overnight. I couldn't believe it. I was all set to start him right over again from the very beginning; but first decided to backtrack just a few books. Luckily, this did the trick; he had simply had a crisis of confidence, an "off" moment – just a blip; and then we were back on course.

At the end of the 120 books, I had a surprise arranged in store. I had visited the local library down the road and primed the staff the day before for a visit; when the man came to my house at the usual time expecting his lesson, he had no idea that this was the final book in the process. Once he had read it successfully, I invited him to hop in the car and I drove him over there. The librarians showed him all around the different areas and he left with a brand new membership card.

For *months* afterwards (until I finally put my foot down and nipped it in the bud) the fella and his mum sent plates of Indian food over to me several times a week – grateful is an understatement. His mind had just opened; and that for me was the greatest reward.

On the day I moved away from the area, I went over to his house to say goodbye. That was the last time I ever saw him.

He was sitting in the window – reading a newspaper...

SO WHY DID I STOP?

There were, in truth, a number of causes. Teaching may indeed be a job in a million, with no two days the same, but it is also one of those careers that will take and take and take from you: no matter how much you do – you can always do more. Few will particularly thank you for doing so – it is a pressure more or less self-imposed out of a sense of guilt, duty, or both; so, as illustrated in my own related episode, this career lends itself to workaholism to an extent not many other vocations can. While pupil or student behaviour can wear you down – it's not so much *what* they're doing, it's the *same*

behaviour, novel to them of course, and often to you at the start! But day after day, year after year, it can become wearing!

I have a friend who will go to SEN schools to be spat on, hit and abused on a daily basis: that takes a very special level of commitment which I admire infinitely but do not myself possess.

A lot of people might paint a rosier picture of the situation and won't tell you the darker sides of the job. I feel it's my duty to do so. Some might be thinking, whoa, you're gonna turn off people reading from ever entering teaching talking like this! Again, I don't see it as my responsibility either to turn anyone on or off it; just telling it like it is. Of course it would be nice if some people do find the general balance and richness of anecdotes inspiring; but then again, if they don't, I am not going to lose sleep over it; what I have portrayed here is real life.

I do firmly believe that, while nothing can replace an expertise borne of decades' experience, Teaching is – and in some ways *should* be – a young person's vocation – there's a time to make way for the next generation; and a very special energy about anyone at the very beginning of their Teaching career. You are young and well, you have boundless energy, you are idealistic, you have the latest cutting edge skills fresh from college; and you are more resilient to the endless grind of admin and paperwork. It was that excessive, increasing workload – not the students – which drove me into supply. You may well think you will *never* fatigue, never wear out, can take steps to avoid doing so, vitamins, mindfulness and exercise; but trust me: it creeps up on you. That first energy does *not* stick around forever; I would urge anyone at the start of their career, if there are particular goals you hope to accomplish, act on them right now, while you have the energy to do so.

The greatest contributory factor by far, which led to my exit from Teaching was the agencies. By and large, these are target-driven, profit-orientated organisations who will happily lie to you to get you to take an assignment; and don't care what kind of lion's den they send you into. Desperate for regular work, I was once even coerced into accepting an assignment which involved driving over 30 miles each way with no fuel allowance – and for £10 less than my normal daily rate – to teach a habitually violent prisoner convicted of GBH. The agent told me to sleep on it, and to call back if I had second thoughts – well, of course I *did* – and she flew into a rage when I turned it down!

By the start of the 21st Century, gone were the glory-days of City-based supply pools, when you could work for one school paying automatically to Teacher's Pay Scale and allowing contributions to Teacher's Pensions. The agencies now rule the roost – they took power in a *vacuum* created by an absence of effective Council co-ordination and management. The 'Golden Age' of supply, in my experience, was from 2003 to 2008 – most of the time I was working four, if not five full days a week. By the end, it was three month periods with no work, each morning dressing up in smart trousers, shirt, tie, polished shoes, waiting for the phone to ring; then at 9.15 taking all the clobber off again. Think about what that does to your self-esteem; the last vestiges of your career confidence. Each week I was either e-mailed, texted or telephoned regarding my "availability" the following week; then, armed with the information given, no work would follow from any of the three agencies I was always registered with. Things would go like this.

"Err, Guy, I'm glad you've called because actually I need to speak to you; I believe you've fallen out of compliance."

"Well, look, the only reason I would have fallen out of compliance is that you haven't given me a single assignment in the last six months."

"Guy... if you'll let me finish" (a favourite phrase of many of these plodding jobsworths armed with their modicum of power), "all we need are the names of couple of referees; we'll do the rest."

I oblige and provide the required contacts. They succeed in speaking to my referees (after six weeks) and I am assured all that is required of me is done. A few days later, I am e-mailed: "In the interests of safeguarding we need you to go online and complete this course in the next seven days; we can't get you out to work if you don't."

I comply, complete the online course which takes over an hour; score 100% in the assessment and inform the branch. Only to then be told, "Guy, we understand you've changed your surname. If you didn't do it by deed poll, just in case we're audited, we need a solicitor's letter confirming that you are legally one and the same person. We can't get you out to work without it."

I ask a London-based solicitor cousin of mine to write me just such a confirmation letter on his firm's headed notepaper as a favour.

Three weeks later it arrives.

"But Guy," says the agent, "did you pay for that letter?"

"Well, no..."

"Well, please would you send us a letter that's been paid for. And the thing is, Guy, you've fallen out of compliance. So we need you to come into the branch and re-register."

I protest that they are just putting one stalling tactic after another in my way.

"How do I know that in another six months, when again you've offered me no work, I won't have "fallen out of compliance" again and we have to go through this whole rigmarole for the umpteenth time? It's like a scene out of Terry Gilliam's *Brazil!*"

"Well if you'd like to speak to the branch manager, maybe that's the best way forward; of course if you'd accept a lower pay-rate, there'd be more chances for us to get you work; the schools just won't pay that..."

The truth: the schools won't pay the *massive* mark-up/profit margin the agencies pile on top of the (already cut) rate the teacher is paid. With the cost of living rising, you can only swallow so many pay cuts!

All this from an agency who were an embarrassing 20 minutes late for a whole set of interviews scheduled by *themselves* – and who never ended up getting me a day's work...

The big chains were even worse. Often they would take on a Council's Education tender in order to secure a much larger general Recruitment contract. They went through the motions on the Education side but actually made little effort to secure work for their teachers. It was impossible to contact my agent in one such firm. The process was even more tortuous than that loathsome shoe-shop "muzak" you have to sit through when you ring HMRC! Every time I rang up, whoever answered would ask me to hold, then come back to the phone with exactly the same stock-phrase:

"Err, he's just got a *sandwich* in his mouth – can I get him to ring you back?"

I'm not a violent man, but by the time I'd heard this "sandwich" line nine or ten times, with no callback, I felt like saying "You tell him, if he doesn't come to the phone right now, I'll shove that non-existent sandwich where the sun don't shine!"

By the end, half the time, I was doing the agencies' work for them, getting bookings by speaking to schools directly, but not getting work 'direct' as the schools preferred to go via their established *agency* arrangement. The agency would then get their substantial cut for having done absolutely nothing proactive to procure me work! But it was either that approach or starve. Occasionally I would make a rare visit to one agency or another only to spot my name lost in a vortex of jammed gobbledegook way down an enormous whiteboard – so it would hardly be the first one seen, or to spring to mind. The truth was, 9 times out of 10 they would always favour a newly qualified teacher – despite the inexperience – because the schools were charged a fixed rate no matter who was sent in. The agency's profit margin would be infinitely higher with an NQT, as they could get away with paying those teachers much less. The only work I was getting was via schools who requested *me* specifically – I must have been doing something right...

Beyond Teaching, however, I did have an unfulfilled dream of my own to achieve. I was sole creator of an animated children's film, *The Man With The Eye At The End Of His Finger*,' which had become nothing less than my life's creative work. Given the infinitesimally slow rate of progress, colouring pixel-by-pixel, the computer I was using, which dated back to the "beige" era was so obsolete, the time would soon come when it would be virtually irreparable if a major problem developed. That, and the realisation that unless I devoted 100% of my time to the project, I could die before finishing it, proved the tipping-point: I had to give up Teaching altogether.

I did so around 18 months prior to the Covid 19 pandemic, which meant, job-status-wise, I was effectively invisible. I wasn't paid PAYE, I wasn't self-employed, I made no money from what I did *and*, as I could claim no benefit (not being a job-seeker), I wasn't even officially *unemployed*. In addition, having sacked the last of my agencies for failing to find me work, I wasn't eligible for the Furlough scheme.

Despite Covid bringing as much suffering, grief and loneliness as it did to so many, Lockdown allowed me to graft away on the film uninterrupted, in complete isolation; and notwithstanding overwhelming technical obstacles I won't go into here, after 27 years, the film was complete at last. It had its World Premiere at the Retro Computer Museum in October 2021 and has gone on to win multiple international awards, on the back of which came the offer of some lecturing days at a well-known local University's Animation degree course. I also have a vector-illustrated children's picture-book adaptation ready for publication. I don't think I'd have been much cop at all that "Remote Teaching" from home anyway; I'd have been way too wary of being caught on camera in a straggly dressing gown, in a room I'd allowed to descend into chaos!

Would I ever go back to teaching though?

Having at one point become a slave to it, up until 2a.m. most nights preparing resources, something in me snapped – I came full circle and have zealously guarded my work/life balance ever since! My level of commitment by the end was... well, I felt I barely had the tip of one toe dipped in the waters of Education... I'll admit to an occasional pang of survivor's guilt, but by and large, I'm very happy.

Despite the undeniable lure of teaching and the awareness you are doing something worthwhile with your life, I very much doubt I would go back – unless purely as a visitor, to tell stories. I've realised money isn't everything; it can be a trap, when it should just be a means to an end. It's more important to have the time to pursue precious creative goals at your own pace without pressure; the freedom *not* to spend all day in a building filled with recycled air; but to lift your head up and hear the birds sing, smell the flowers, swim a mile each morning and spend precious "loving-time" with a mischievous Labrador – such things are priceless.

But *never* say never!